"*Be Not Conformed* is a wonderfully refreshing book — a powerful affirmation that American culture has the vision and capacity for deep transformation."

— James Conlon, Program Director, Institute in Culture & Creation Spirituality

"*Be Not Conformed* lives up to its title. It clearly shows practical alternatives for living in a way other than the world and the dollar prescribe. But more than that, it lays bare the source of the bones of contention that have riven American society almost since its inception. What makes this combination thoughtbook and workbook unique, however, it its lack of rancor and railing, its thoughtful belief that, if we know what differences to make we can make a difference.

"Only occasionally does a book appear that puts the right names on the things we see and feel. John and Kristi Culley have crafted just such a book about our country. Their prose is clean and direct, their passion is clear, and over and over again they untangle the knots that tie us all up in contradictory beliefs and acts. They show us ways to grow, to heal, to enhance the body politic and mend the fabric of our world. Theirs is a book that goes beyond anger into effective care. A wise, compassionate, helpful book."

— Robert H. Conn, Director, Office of Public Policy Programs, Division of Higher Education, United Methodist Church

"Kristi and John Culley have given us a book that is both idealistic and practical. They trace the evil that good people do to our failure to realize our own intrinsic worth — finally to our lack of faith. In a competitive and individualistic age, they point us back to the values on which true community is based and show us how to revive them."

— Richard Wood, President, Earlham College, Richmond, Indiana

"When I finished this book I sent it to my grandson. The most important person I know."

— Will D. Campbell, author of *Brother to a Dragonfly*

"Simple. Straightforward. Direct. An honest unmasking of the dysfunctional values and belief system we in the United States live out daily. *Be Not Conformed* invites the reader to explore new possibilities for understanding and enhancing human worth, work, and community.

"This book provides energetic and joyful answers to the question, 'What difference can one person make?'

"If you are searching for creative ways to enhance the quality of your life — and to heal a part of the larger world at the same time — this book will prove to be an invaluable resource."

— Helen R. Neinast, Director,
Campus Ministry Section, United Methodist Church

BE NOT CONFORMED

Be not conformed to this world
but be transformed by the renewal of your mind,
that you may prove what is the will of God,
what is good and acceptable and perfect.

ROMANS 12:2

BE NOT CONFORMED

CHANGING THE WAY WE SEE THE WORLD

John Culley
and
Kristi Culley

Published in the United States by Meyer-Stone Books,
a division of Meyer, Stone, and Company, Inc.,
2014 South Yost Avenue, Bloomington, IN 47403
Telephone: 812-333-0313

Cover design: Carol Evans-Smith

Typesetting output: TEXSource, Houston

Manufactured in the United States of America
93 92 91 90 89 5 4 3 2 1

Library of Congress Cataloging in Publication Data

Culley, John, 1930-
Be not conformed : changing the way we see the world / John Culley and Kristi Culley.
p. cm.
Bibliography: p.
ISBN 0-940989-45-X
1. Social values. 2. Values — United States. United States — Social conditions — 1980- 4. Religion. I. Culley, Kristi, 1964- .
II. Title.
HM73.C82 1989
303.3'72 — dc19 88-43050
CIP

To Barbara (Mom), Katie, Jennifer, and Josh,
with thanks for reading innumerable drafts and renditions,
for eating around the stacks of papers
that sat on the dining room table for months,
and especially for your support, encouragement,
and unconditional love.

Contents

Preface

Sociologist Peter Berger describes a kind of event in a person's life that he calls "alternation." This event is an experience through which we gain a new perspective on society or the world in general. Berger says this event can reveal society as "something radically different from what had been previously taken for granted."[1]

We are all socialized to view society in a certain way and most of us tend to feel, because of this socialization, that society can be no other way. "Yet this consciousness of what Alfred Schutz has called the 'world taken for granted' is not of such solidity that it cannot be breached." Once such a breach occurs, the world seems different to us with "new dimensions and colors." Whenever the breach comes quickly, "it marks the day after which life will never be the same again."[2]

This book offers you the possibility for an experience of alternation. It develops and explores three basic steps in the process of gaining such a new perspective. First, it attempts to breach the world taken for granted through observing and evaluating the social values of the United States from an uncommon perspective. This perspective is the understanding of human worth and significance in our society. Second, it offers an alternative view of human worth and explores the "new dimensions and colors" that could result. Third, it suggests how to live in "the day after which life will never be the same again."

We strongly believe that there is a vital need for such a process resulting in widespread alternation in our society. We are faced with a multitude of problems and dangers, many of them critical, that stem from taking our view of the world for granted. Here we attempt to question that view, to reveal society for what it is, and begin to formulate a new vision that is more functional, creative, and humane.

This book is not offered as a definitive answer but as a beginning. It is up to each reader to develop these ideas into a new vision that offers hope for healing and can be an effective force for change.

CHAPTER 1

The Need for an Alternative Worldview

For the first time in history the physical survival of the human race depends on a radical change of the human heart.
— Erich Fromm

Once upon a time, so the story goes, the Emperor claimed to have new clothes. He was proud of his clothiers, boastful of his clothes, and paraded around so all could see his marvelous clothes. And everyone agreed with him, and made a big fuss, and felt he must be right because he was, of course, the Emperor. Something didn't seem quite right, however, even to the Emperor. Somehow the actual situation, the naked truth, didn't quite live up to all the claiming and boasting. But the people weren't really sure whether they should mention this fact or not.

Many years later there was a nation that claimed, as nations love to do, to be the greatest nation on earth. But something didn't seem quite right. Somehow the actual situation didn't quite live up to all the claiming and boasting....

We Americans like to think that we are the greatest society in the world and take pride in the "American way of life," yet each year we have 5000 teenage suicides and many more runaway children. We have 45,000 deaths on our roadways, a major crime every two seconds, and an unknown number of people addicted to alcohol, tranquilizers, nicotine, and other drugs.

We take pride in being the wealthiest country on earth, yet it is estimated that one out of five American children lives in poverty. We claim to have the highest standard of living on earth and wish that all people could do as well. However, in order to have that standard of living, our 6 percent of the world's population must use approximately 30 percent of the world's resources expended each year.

Americans sincerely wish for peace, yet we continue to be involved in armed conflicts, and we rank first in selling arms to the world. We speak of the need for all nations to work together, but we use "national interests" as the basis for our relations with other countries. Schooling is so valuable to us that we make it compulsory, yet we allow one-sixth of us to be functionally illiterate. We want our children to have the needed skills of cooperation, yet we inundate them with models and experiences of competition.

We talk about the advantages of individualism, yet we have a strong tendency to conform to the economic, political, social, and academic expectations of our socio-economic class. On the one hand, we say that the individual is to be valued as he or she is. On the other hand, we push ourselves and our children to prove that we can have more, know more, or do better than others.

We seriously believe that we are a good-natured, friendly people, yet 23,000 of us are murdered, and hundreds of thousands of wives, husbands, children, and parents are physically abused each year. We are sensitive to the hungry in our own country and around the world, yet we pay our farmers to raise less food in order to control prices.

We believe in the importance of community and we value the responsibility an individual has to the community, yet each year millions of us break the law (in traffic, in filing tax returns, in white-collar crime), acting for our own good against the good of the community. We believe in government by the people, yet rarely do more than 60 percent of those registered go to the polls in any election. We believe in individual liberty for all people, yet we often support authoritarian regimes throughout the world.

Such inconsistencies often leave us feeling confused about our national goals and values and at a loss as to how to resolve or even cope with the problems that result. If we still suffer from inequality, violence, and poverty when we have tried to be just, peaceful, and democratic, is there really anything we can do? Our societal inconsistencies thus cause confusion and apathy. More critically, they also prevent us from making reasonable, rational decisions concerning social needs, political policy, and economic and scientific development. If we are not clear about our values and goals, our decisions will most likely be haphazard and undirected.

This is not to say that the decisions that have been made in this nation throughout its history have gotten us nowhere. We have developed into a world power with incredible political and economic influence. We like to think we have the potential for "unlimited" progress and growth. But what is less certain are the benefits and positive results of such development. With no solid, consistent understanding of what is valued and what is not, we have often rushed blindly and rashly to advance one value while neglecting or even destroying another.

The constant push for progress has gotten out of control. The promise of technology blinds us to the need for humane, rational thinking, planning, and decision-making. Our ethics and understanding have not kept pace with our technological advancements. Therefore we neither know how to use our progress humanely nor take heed of the possible consequences and side-effects.

Nuclear power, pesticides, strip mining, off-shore drilling—we eagerly welcomed these and other "advances" as ways to overcome obstacles to progress and production. But by focusing only on our present needs and specific problems we failed to take into account that any change in a closed environment will have repercussions throughout the eco-system. Like Pandora opening her tantalizing box, we have set loose processes beyond our understanding and control, processes with long-range consequences we are just beginning to realize.

A change of some sort is inevitable, for such a situation is not likely to remain stable for long. We cannot, without disaster, continue to use up resources, pollute the eco-system, and threaten each other with thousands of nuclear warheads forever. We must either change purposely in an expressed attempt to create a more humane world or the situation will change without us. And the result of that change would probably be far from humane.

Symptomism

We have met the enemy and he is us.
—Pogo

The declaration that all is not right and something must be done about it is hardly news to most Americans. Many have been aware of this need for change and have struggled for years to bring it about. We have tried new programs, new leaders, gallant crusades. And yet, despite brief gains and small successes, we are still faced with seemingly insurmountable problems.

We are suffering from "symptomism"—fervently treating the symptoms while doing little or nothing about the cause. Such solutions may seem to help for awhile, but without attacking the root of the problem they can never be successful. The problems spring up again with new and often more widespread symptoms.

A prime example of symptomism in our society is the American penchant for following fad diets while maintaining a sedentary lifestyle. Another, more tragic, example is the practice of selling infant formula to "help" malnourished babies in underdeveloped nations without making it possible for their mothers to have disease-free water with which to mix the formula. The good intentions are there, but only treating the symptoms without looking any deeper does nothing to alleviate the problem.

It has been said that you cannot do away with violence by using violence and there is no way to peace except through peace. We cannot hope that the very thing that threatens us will save us. Yet that is what we do. We think that if we just return to the ways of our past, to our traditional values, then all will be well. We fail to realize that it was these very ways that led us to where we are now. We try more extreme forms of what we already have and are surprised when no positive change results.

Many movements and revolutions have failed because of such symptomism. The changes didn't go deep enough to affect the paradigm, the underlying blueprint, the DNA of the culture. After all the furor and bloodshed nothing really changed.

This is what happened to Soviet Communism. The Russian revolution had far-reaching goals and enacted sweeping reforms, but ultimately it brought about little change in the basic structure of society. The only real political change was who was in power; the dream of a classless society, of a true communism, was not realized.

The same occurred with the independence movement in Latin America. Simon Bolivar led a successful attempt to free the continent from colonial rule. After the Spanish pulled out, however, there were no structures left for ruling the countries. To avert disaster Bolivar set in charge the only organized section of society, the military — and it has been there ever since. The only real change was who was in power.

Our country has been similarly plagued by symptomism, although maybe not so dramatically. Our policies and plans are fraught with examples of treating the symptoms while ignoring the cause. We have a welfare system that provides a subsistence to those below the poverty level but does nothing to attack the reason we have poverty in such a rich nation. After forty years of welfare we have not eliminated poverty. Instead, more and more citizens are in need of aid.

We elect leaders who are strong and "successful" in hopes that they will bring about needed changes. We do not seem to realize that they are successful because they work within the system — the very system we need them to change. Even the strongest and most charismatic are not likely to pull the ladder out from under themselves, or even realize that another way is possible. Instead they provide us with more programs that address only the surface of the problem. Thus despite electing new leaders we often end up with the same processes, goals, and perspectives.

Symptomism makes us feel we are doing something while, in reality, we are not addressing the problem at all. If you are allergic to ice cream, it won't help to try different flavors. If our worldview is dysfunctional, it won't help to use it to solve our problems. If we insist on working out of the old understanding, we will continue to utilize the very attitudes and patterns that caused the problems in the first place.

The sort of change required is as profound as the problems facing us. The paradigm on which our society is based has become dysfunctional. What we must do is alter the very way we look at and understand ourselves. We must change our worldview.

The Adaptability of Worldviews

Truths are illusions of which one has forgotten that they are illusions. — Jacques Derrida

Webster defines "worldview" as "one's philosophy or conception of the universe and of life." This is a good definition, but a bit too simple to suggest the complexities and the pervasiveness of a worldview. More completely, a worldview is a complex system of attitudes, values, and perceptions of reality that form the implicit and explicit structure of a culture. It is a web of interrelated parts, each affecting and influencing the other, that provides both the framework and the motivating factors of how we live our lives, what we understand life to be like, and what role we have in the world.

Each culture has its own way of seeing the world, its own frame of reference by which it understands what is going on. This understanding is more than likely subconscious and seems to the individual like common sense. We assume that it describes reality, the way the world is. The fact that these worldviews have been found to differ widely between cultures hints that what we call "reality" may be more complex and filled with more alternatives than we might have imagined.

Worldviews, like species, are adapted to their particular circumstance. If that circumstance changes they must adapt in order to survive. Since a worldview is only our perception of reality, what we think of as reality is not as concrete and immutable as it might seem.

Many times through history we have changed our idea of what the world is like. Often the change has been in small steps, but our fundamental ideas, our worldview, our paradigm of reality has also changed dramatically at times. At one time it was accepted as fact that the earth was flat and the sun and stars revolved around it. At another time the divine right of kings was held to be true in most European cultures. Slavery was understood by its defenders as God's will. Questioning these beliefs was seen as heretical or silly — why doubt the way things are? But slowly these ideas changed and were replaced by new ones, and the worldview changed.

Such a change in worldview does not mean that the worldview was "wrong" and was then corrected. Worldviews are not more or less wrong or right. They are more of less functional. If a worldview satisfactorily explains what is going on, if the explanation works in the situation and for the people, then it is functional.

Problems arise when the conditions change and the worldview is no longer able to explain what is happening and can give no clear or helpful understanding of how to deal with the situation. At this point the worldview becomes dysfunctional and must either change or become contradictory and flawed. This is what happened when

Copernicus declared the sun to be the center of the solar system and when Columbus sailed across the Atlantic and didn't fall off the edge of the earth. The worldview had to change to include the new information.

There are times when people don't adapt their worldview. This results in confusion and perhaps destruction of the society. Examples can be found throughout history. When Cortez landed in Mexico with little more than a handful of men, the Aztecs were faced with a situation totally outside their experience. In order to understand what was happening, they reached inside the old worldview and found an explanation that proved to be tragically dysfunctional. Cortez's arrival became understandable as the return of the god Quetzalcoatl. When the Aztecs realized their mistake it was too late to stop the military conquest. The inability to change their idea of reality kept the Aztecs from seeing the danger that threatened them.

We are seemingly experiencing a similar inability to adapt our perception of reality. Alvin Toffler tells of asking a group of bright teenagers to make a list of their predictions of the future. When no personal references showed up among the predictions, he asked them to make another list, this time for their own personal lives. He found that the two lists were logically incompatible. Whereas the general predictions pointed to a turbulent time ahead, the personal predictions showed that the turbulence would have little, if any, effect on the individuals. In spite of predictions of world wars, widespread famine, depressions, and shortages of resources, individual plans to graduate, get a good job, marry, and settle down would be realized on schedule.

"No matter how turbulent a world they pictured,... the way of life foreseen for themselves as individuals seldom differed from the way of life possible in the present.... The respondents ... made no provision for change in themselves, no provision for adaptation to a world exploding with change."[1]

Personal teaching experiences with junior college classes bear out Toffler's complaint. Most of the students who wrote scenarios of the future had trouble breaking out of the myth of the American dream of success. Their awareness of economic and political problems in our nation and around the world had little effect on their continuing belief that they could live the good life.

Such attitudes suggest that we realize the situation around us is changing but we are failing to adapt our worldview to be functional in the new environment. Like the Aztecs, we are faced with a threatening situation totally outside our experience. If we continue attempting to explain what is going on from our old perspective we will not adapt and we will not survive.

Changing Our Worldview

We must remyth our world!... Our old dream has become a nightmare; we must dream a better dream.
—Elizabeth Dodson Gray

What we need is a profound change, a change that will get to the root of the problem. We need to see that our worldview, our cultural paradigm is not functional in the situation we face. We must be willing to change, to adapt to a new situation in order to survive, to enter into the process of changing our worldview. Any lesser change will not get to the source of the problem.

There are three important steps in the process of changing a worldview. The first is becoming aware of our worldview. It is not easy to do, to become aware of something so pervasive and ubiquitous; it is much like a fish becoming aware of the water. But if the fish is in a polluted stream it must somehow "realize" that the water is the source of its problem and swim to another, cleaner area. Similarly we must become aware of our worldview in order to realize the threat it poses and attempt to change the situation.

The second step is to realize that there are other possibilities, that our dysfunctional worldview does not have to be "the way life is." There are other perceptions of reality, other ways of seeing and understanding the world and the role of humans within that world. Once we are freed from the perspective of the past, we can begin to creatively imagine new possibilities. This process is called envisioning.

The final stage of changing a worldview is the act of trusting, acting on the new vision of what could be. Courageously stepping out of the old worldview, we can "try the new one on for size." It is at this point that a new way of being and understanding can be made real and dynamic.

See below chapter 15, "Food for Thought," pp. 168ff., nos. 9, 29, and 44.

CHAPTER 2

Two Americas

White man speaks with forked tongue.

Becoming aware of our worldview involves taking a close look at our society. We must try to determine what lies behind the social structure and behaviors: What is our interpretation of reality? How do we think the world works? How does this affect our lives? We must look at our values because values are based on a fundamental understanding of what life is about and what is of ultimate importance for us.

Values can often be unexamined. Thus, it is important that we take into account both explicit values (the values we claim and consciously hold) and implicit values (what our behavior indicates we value). Both sorts of values can shed light on what our worldview is like. However, at this point we may encounter a problem. As noted at the beginning of chapter 1, American society is fraught with inconsistencies. What we say and what we do are not necessarily congruent. What we claim to want and what we actually work for sometimes conflict. We may claim to value peace, equality, and generosity. But if we build for war, continue to allow discrimination, and have an economy built to a great extent on greed, it seems obvious that we must value these as well. It seems that our explicit and implicit values are contradictory.

Having contradictory values is a significant characteristic of American society and has been so since the beginning of the nation. Persons who came to these shores for religious freedom often denied that freedom to others. Our Founding Fathers, struggling for independence, refused that independence to slaves and, to some extent, the Founding Mothers. From our earliest days we have been evangelistic about the right of nations to self-determination, yet have pursued policies that eradicated many of the Native American cultures and caused us to intervene continually in the affairs of other countries.

Michael Novak, Roman Catholic social observer, sees that our values have had contrary tendencies from the beginning. We are a strange mixture of obedience and lawlessness, of praising equality while practicing inequality, of being humble yet proud of our being the greatest nation on earth.[1]

Barbara Lupo of Clergy and Laity Concerned says, "This is no longer 'one nation, under God.' It is *two* nations. Two very different Americas. One based on arrogance and a false sense of superiority. The other based on ethical, biblical principles—the principles on which this nation was founded."[2]

Senator William Fulbright likewise sees two American traditions. One causes us to be generous and humane; the other produces narrow egotism. On the one hand we are self-critical and on the other we are self-righteous. In the use of great power we will be judicious in one situation and arrogant in another.[3]

Theologian L. Harold DeWolf also identifies two traditional, but contradictory, value systems. He says our thoughts and actions are affected by both "America A" and "America B." America A is "generous, community-minded, benevolent, and humane." It maintains that there should be "no discrimination on grounds of religion or race, and that justice and peace should be sought with self-restraint, patience, care for the truth, and generous consideration of others." America B, on the other hand, is "tight-fisted, individualistic, self-righteous, materialistic, aggressive, impatient, vindictive, and prone to violence." It is also "quick to resort to arms." America B is not a mere failure to live according to the values of America A but is deliberately promoted as a system contrary to America A. "That they *are* contrary is too seldom realized."[4]

W. L. Miller, in *Of Thee, Nevertheless, I Sing,* says it is possible to develop a picture of American history "in which the two large traditions compete: the tradition of growing democratic inclusiveness and humane action for social justice" and the tradition "of competition, free enterprise, individualism, the market." The second tradition is the stronger in our culture in spite of persistent manifestations of the first.[5]

These two traditions are not only different; they contradict each other. They have thus been in constant conflict throughout the history of our society. We are usually unaware that we have two traditions of values and therefore unaware of the conflict between them. Not realizing this problem, we attempt to adhere to all the values, as if they were compatible. We become inconsistent when we claim values from one tradition while acting on those from the other.

In order to get a clear understanding of our worldview we must first look at both of the traditions from a historical perspective. It is important to realize that specific groups or individuals did not totally espouse one tradition or the other. The shapers of our society were influenced by both traditions, much as we are today. However, certain groups and movements tended to emphasize one tradition or the other as they tried to follow their beliefs and act on their values. By looking at the impact and development of these historical factors we can trace the influence of the two traditions.

The First Tradition

> *Our ideal... is embodied in a voluntary community where mutuality exists, where goods are shared, and which is "glued together" by a common cause, warmed at the fire of a vision.* —James Sellers

The first tradition developed from seventeenth-century religious thought, selected Enlightenment philosophy interpreted during the time of the American Revolution, and various communal experiments in the eighteenth and nineteenth centuries that developed in response to what was felt to be rampant individualism.

Each influence contributed (1) an idea about the nature of the best possible community, the development of which became the goal, (2) a model for a corporate cooperative agreement that would guarantee the establishment and maintenance of such a community, and (3) patterns of responsible behavior necessary to fulfill the agreement.

Religious Influence

Two groups that helped develop this first tradition were the Puritans and the Quakers. They were very active during the founding years of the colonies in the early 1600s and thus had a strong influence on our ideas of what it means to be a citizen. Although there were many theological points where they differed considerably, they each strongly encouraged the responsible interdependence of individual and community.

The purpose of the Puritan effort was to serve God. The Puritans thought this could best be done by developing a model Christian community, envisioned as a "City upon a Hill," which would be seen and emulated by all the world. The building of that community was their goal.

Since Puritanism held that human beings are naturally sinful and prone to selfishness, government had to be limited so that no one person or group would have total power over the community. On the other hand, each individual was a valued child of God and thus should be capable of participating responsibly with other members of the community. It followed that government could be empowered by the consent of the citizens, with each citizen having a say in determining rules and policies. To guarantee this, the people signed a written agreement called a "covenant," which, among other things, called for genuine cooperation and defined the rights and responsibilities for the good of each and all. The only ones who could sign the covenant were those whose hearts had been changed by God and thus had the will to do what was right and responsible.[6]

Ideally, because of the God-changed heart, individuals would voluntarily behave in such ways as to strengthen the community. They believed that they should be responsible for each other, not because of any selfish reward, but because "binding oneself to the others and to the common good is, *in itself,* a worthwhile act, and its own reward."[7]

The Quakers understood this caring for the general welfare very clearly. They envisioned an ideal community in which all persons would be equal before the sight of God and equal before each other. Such a society would be guided by personal revelation known as the "inner light of God." The behaviors flowing from the "inner light" included the respect of all fellow human beings as God's children, a strong commitment to freedom of conscience for all, and works of civic responsibility to all levels of the community.

Although the influence of the Quakers on American values is

not as well known as that of the Puritans, it has had its impact through the years in various efforts on behalf of immigrants, the poor, and the uneducated. While the Quakers had control over the policies of the colony of Pennsylvania, there were no troubles between them and the Native Americans living in the area. "They were even further ahead of their time in believing that Christ's highest precepts led toward peace, not a sword; toward fair and honorable dealings with the Indian; and toward freedom for the African slave."[8]

The Enlightenment

A second source of the first tradition is the Enlightenment. The political leaders of the late colonial period, our Founding Fathers, were greatly influenced by the writings of the philosophers Hobbes, Locke, Montesquieu, Voltaire, and Rousseau. These philosophers wrestled with the questions of what it means to be a state and on what basis any government can claim authority. From extensive reading and much debating among themselves, the Founding Fathers concluded that the purpose of government is to ensure "life, liberty, and the pursuit of happiness" for the individual. This was based on the radical concept that "all men are created equal."

In reaction to the insensitivity of the Crown, they set as their goal the founding of a community of liberty. The word "liberty" became the rallying cry for the American Revolution and has since been regarded as the chief of our values, even though the word "freedom" has replaced it in general use.

The agreement that guarantees liberty is an established social contract. The contract exists so that all citizens, including the leaders, can cooperate in maintaining the rights and responsibilities that preserve liberty. The first formal social contract for the new country was the Articles of Confederation. The second was the Constitution, which went into effect in 1789.

A social contract will not provide liberty, however, if there is no sense of interdependence among the citizens. This necessary behavior is what the political philosopher Montesquieu called *"la vertu,"* often translated as "civic virtue." This term can be defined as that internally motivated effort by each citizen to put public good ahead of private interests.

Communal Experiments

A third source of the first tradition is the various communal experiments that both preceded and followed national independence. The dream that the early Puritans had of establishing the "City upon a Hill" faded under the press of the constant flow of new arrivals who did not share the Puritan vision of community. The political ideal of "civic virtue" was overwhelmed by the excitement of the self-interest of the market place and the expanding frontier.

In reaction to the highly individualistic social environment, various persons at different times sought to try again to found the ideal community. Groups such as Brook Farm, the Oneida Community, the Amish, and the Shakers established small communities dedicated to interdependence and responsible cooperation. The agreement guaranteeing such a community was the common vision of what the society should be. The behavior that kept the vision fresh was the voluntary commitment of the participants to be responsible to each other.

The voluntary joining was prompted by the quality of personal relationships possible in small, congenial groups. This has to do with a sense of equality and face-to-face encounters that are so often hard to find in the larger society with its patterns of self-interest and competition. In the communal view, there is offered "the claim that community is built up out of the mutuality between us, which introduces a new reality greater than the wills, or the hopes, of either of us taken separately."[9]

Geo-Communocentrism

These sources of the first tradition all have a vision of the good society and a strong sense of interdependence. Each sees the necessity for active cooperation and responsible behavior growing out of a deep inner commitment in order to achieve the common goal.

The threads of this tradition have been and continue to be manifest in the reconstructing of burned barns for neighbors, the building of roadside churches for the use of several denominations, town meetings to work out common problems, responsible cooperation in the face of natural disasters, and the development of united agencies to care for those who need physical or spiritual help.

The values of interdependence, cooperation, and responsibility have continued to inform our private and public discourse to this day. No matter how far from these ideals we fall, we know that without them to guide us we would not long remain a viable society. No matter how much self-serving and competition enters our decision-making, we are sensitive to the values of the first tradition without which we would disintegrate as a nation.

The strength and persistence of this tradition have enabled it to continue to grow and adapt to new situations in our society. Recently, the discourse about community-centered values has increasingly included the whole world in its scope as we realize that we are faced with worldwide ecological and economic problems. We enter cooperative efforts with other countries, sometimes at our expense, to try to protect endangered species, curtail acid rain, question the clear-cutting of the rain forests, and stop the erosion of the ozone layer in the upper atmosphere. It is being realized that a communocentric worldview cannot be limited to small communities or to human beings because everything is interdependent with everything else. Communocentrism, in order to be fully effective in our day, must be expanded in its scope and understood in terms of the global community.

Thus the first tradition can be understood as "geo-communocentric," emphasizing the communocentric values of interdependence, cooperation, and responsibility, and focusing on the world as a community.

The Second Tradition

We Americans have never had a genuine politics — that is, something apart from economics that gives direction to our community life. Instead, American politics has been but a reflection of its laissez-fair economic system. . . . Indeed, American political history is but the record of a more or less amicable squabble over the division of the spoils of a growing economy.

— William Ophuls

Individualism

The second tradition has two themes. One developed from the ideas and energies of those who thought that the ideal community was one that offered individuals a chance to pursue their own self-interest. For every person who came to the New World to establish some kind of interdependent society, there were vast numbers who came to carve out their own personal destiny unhindered by the political, economic, and geographical restrictions of Europe. The pursuit of self-interest was usually manifest in the search for economic gain.

It was inevitable that a strong sense of autonomy became a popular value in our culture. The settlers had to learn to manage on their own. People had to rely on their own skills because there were not enough people on the frontier to allow specialization. They learned to govern themselves because the government in the mother country was too far away. Long before the Revolution developed, personal independence was highly valued.

Ironically, even the community-minded Puritans encouraged individualism by insisting that each person should be able to read and interpret the scriptures for himself or herself. This led to schisms in theology as well as within communities. Many in the Puritan tradition were attracted by a greatly modified form of Calvinism that rejected predestination and held that salvation could be assured for oneself by living a respectable life and doing good works.

This theology appealed to the individualistic pioneer and paved the way for the growth of pietism. A subjective expression of faith, pietism arose in Europe as a rejection of creedal orthodoxy. It swept into the colonies with the Great Awakening and set the style for religion in this nation until the present. It stresses a private, individual relationship to God, and understands sin and grace in purely personal terms.[10]

The privatization of religion was but one manifestation of self-interest in the New World. The social, political, and economic areas of life were also privatized as people strove for success in some kind of competitive process. Success can be won in thousands of human enterprises: arm wrestling, land speculation, gambling, telling lies, crafts, politics, sex, business, gold prospecting. There can be no private, personal success, however, without the necessary and socially expected behavior known as individual initiative. Success may not come as a result of individual initiative, but no success is possible without it. The "self-made man" is a value in our heritage that endures to this day.

Prosperity

The other theme of the second tradition is prosperity. Prosperity does not necessarily mean the attaining of great wealth; it can mean whatever is economically significant to the individual: "a comfortable living," land to pass along to the children, old age security, a lifestyle equal, or superior, to one's peers, political and social influence.

The search for prosperity on these shores began when the first explorers sought new trade routes and cities of gold. Colonies were developed in order to supply raw materials that could be turned into goods or sold directly to bring gold into the private and governmental treasuries of the mother country. Far more colonists came to the New World to seek their fortune than came to worship in their own way. Even those who came to find freedom from religious persecution discovered that the New World offered exciting economic opportunities as well. A cartoon shows Pilgrims aboard the *Mayflower.* One says to the other, "Sure, I'm going for religious freedom but my long-range goal is real estate." Sermons preached by Puritan ministers condemning land speculation indicate that the cartoon has a historical basis.

Free Enterprise

The traditional means to prosperity is the economic system that we call "free enterprise." This system had been known for centuries, but it was not until 1776 that Adam Smith published his *Wealth of Nations* and gave free enterprise its formal philosophical basis. Considering the impact this book has had on our culture, it would be appropriate to celebrate that year as much for the book as for the Declaration of Independence.

Smith wrote that society would be best served if each individual acted in terms of self-interest. In order for people to enhance themselves economically, each should make the best possible product and sell it as cheaply as possible. This method would bring buyers to the door and money to the pockets. With each person making the best possible product and selling at the lowest possible price, everyone would benefit. An "invisible hand" would guide the economy to the interests of all. The community was to be enhanced, not by cooperative efforts, but by competition.

It was understood that the free enterprise system will not function unless each individual is diligent about his or her work. This attitude was undergirded by the so-called Puritan ethic, which developed, in part, out of Calvinist theology. Originally, the Calvinists thought of work as a manifestation of faith. One was to glorify God in work as well as in worship. Life was to be simple and frugal. If wealth resulted, it was considered a sign of God's favor. Being poor was not necessarily a sign of God's disfavor, but human proclivities made it easy to suspect this. Few wanted to be thought of as being out of favor with God, so most gave themselves to work to assure their own status now and, it was hoped, in the life to come.

This view has also been called the "Protestant ethic" because the Puritans were not the only Calvinists in the colonies. It is estimated that by the time of the Revolution just under half of the population were Calvinists of some kind. This number included the Scotch-Irish, the Pennsylvania Germans known as the "Dutch," the Huguenots, the Dutch Reformed Church, and various English sect groups as well as New England Congregationalists who developed out of the Puritan tradition. Their influence was probably greater than their numbers would indicate because their view of work and prosperity fit neatly with the idea of personal independence so important to frontier life.[11]

As this theology became secularized, it became known as the "work ethic." Benjamin Franklin became identified as the leading advocate of this philosophy as he offered pithy admonitions that sound much like the Book of Proverbs: "The sleeping fox catches no poultry"; "The used key is always bright"; "A penny saved is a penny earned." The work ethic emphasizes that if people work hard and save their money they will amount to something. Through work self-interest will be served.

Conforming to this work ethic is the way Americans have most often sought the realization of self-interest. Individual worth and recognition could be gained by becoming prosperous. Success could be gained through competition in the free enterprise system. Of course, this had been recognized ever since the concepts of self-importance and wealth merged in the human mind. The difference in the American story is that prosperity and self-esteem were deemed possible by everyone who would work, not just the nobly born and the powerful.

Tutored by the popular theology of work, people assumed that prosperity came to those who worked for it; and no one should be ashamed of honest economic success. Long before the twentieth century, the people took for granted that "the business of America is business." Free enterprise, at least the American version, should be the way of life for all. The work ethic was the expected social behavior and shame was heaped on those who did not work. It was, and still is, a popular opinion that in resource-rich America only the lazy and sinful go hungry.

These values, however, are not the only ones in the second worldview. As conditions changed across the years other values were added that are not a part of our older traditions. What is not realized by many is that some of the newer values undercut the older ones.

Corporate Capitalism

Just before the Civil War, the free enterprise system began to change from a pattern of individual entrepreneurs and family-owned industries to ever-larger companies and corporations. The war economy propelled American industry into a period of hectic industrial expansion. Those who ruled the giant corporations were no longer content with prosperity. For these men economic success was easily attained and therefore did not bestow the significance it once had. They went after a new goal, the acquiring and using of great power: power over rival industries, power over political systems, power over foreign policy through which they would be insured power over foreign markets.

Power was made possible by "corporate capitalism" with its control of jobs, investments, and subsidiary businesses. From that post-war time, known to some as the "gilded age" and to others as "the Great Barbecue," it was no longer appropriate to speak of American industry as private enterprise, at least not in the sense associated with the image of Benjamin Franklin. The family-owned industries of 1800 had far less impact on the general community than the giant corporations of a hundred years later, which came to influence greatly, if not totally control, markets, the number and quality of jobs, the press, and the politicians.

For the vast majority of people, however, power was completely out of the question. It was their role to work within the system in a shop, factory, accounting office, or other place removed from the centers of power. They were encouraged to believe that being a part of the machinery of American industrial power gave them significance that in earlier times was gained by individual initiative.

In the earlier free enterprise model associated with Franklin, work was understood to be the way to success, self-esteem, and prosperity. In the industrial model in which people competed with each other for wages, work was not a fulfilling activity that gave some meaning to life. It became a necessary, and often disheartening, activity in order to get money to live from week to week.

Consumer Economy

When we speak of traditional values we know that prosperity is still a goal for many, but in spite of individual initiative and hard work our possibilities are controlled to a great extent by the condition of the economy, including the stock market, the money market, and the balance of trade. Free enterprise, in the early sense, is now found only in small business at local levels, and even these cannot escape the power of corporations when ordering stock or pricing goods. We like to believe that the backbone of our economy is simple free enterprise, but it exists only in our national mythology.

It is now understood that without a strong economy there is really no power at all. In order to have a sound economy we must have economic growth. This is the present goal that supersedes all others. Without growth we stagnate. Without growth there is no chance for sharing the "economic pie." Growth means jobs and a favorable balance of trade. Growth means being able to have both guns and butter. If we are to maintain our standard of living and have international influence and prestige, the economy must grow. But how to maintain infinite economic growth with non-renewable resources and the need for population control is a problem with no easy answers.

Finding these answers has become the primary role of our national government. The United States is no longer a political entity supported by an economic process. Rather, it is an economic entity supported by a political process. The economic system is so complex it is felt by many that only a relatively few people have the training and expertise to provide economic and, hence, political leadership. We have become dependent upon these "technologists" who have the required esoteric knowledge and skills we trust will make the economy function to our benefit.

These technologists say that in our need for continuous economic growth our individual self-interest can best be served, not by the work ethic but by the consumer ethic. In order to consume we must have production, but if we produce and do not buy, the economy will founder.

As once we conformed to the idea that our self-interest was best served by vigorous competition for prosperity, so today we conform to the idea that our self-interest is best served by competition in consuming.

It used to be that people worked to save enough to buy what they wanted. Today, such a policy would strangle the economy and send us into a depression. The behavior needed and expected now is "buy now, pay later." The time payment plan has seriously eroded the work ethic.

Those who have not understood the nature of the development of the consumer ethic and still think in terms of the old work ethic are bothered by programs such as welfare, unemployment insurance, and Medicaid. They feel it is somehow un-American to rescue those who ought to be out working for what they get. They misunderstand the pragmatism of such public policy. They do not realize that welfare recipients help keep the economy going by spending money that, under the work ethic philosophy, they don't deserve and wouldn't have. Such programs also create huge systems of administrators, social workers, clerks, drivers, etc. All these people make their living attending to the welfare clientele. Since they receive money for their work they are able to consume.

Oddly enough, crime and other forms of violence also contribute to the Gross National Product. Stolen goods bring money that can be spent. Lawyers get paid as do the court and penal officials. Ambulance and emergency room personnel, police, insurance adjustors, auto repair companies all receive money that can then be used to consume. Even bankruptcy adds to the consuming, with its call for record-keepers, repossessors, lawyers, and court personnel. Wealth is not needed, just the constant movement of goods and services.

Econo-Egocentrism

A growth economy and an overwhelming emphasis on individual gain are the primary characteristics of the second tradition. The worldview that expresses this tradition stresses conformity, competition, and self-interest. We shall call this worldview "econo-egocentrism."

See below chapter 15, "Food for Thought," pages 168ff., nos. 7, 54, and 55.

CHAPTER 3

What Are You Worth?

Respect... it's not something you're born with; it's something you earn.

—U.S. Marine Corps commercial

Becoming aware of our worldview begins with dissecting it and looking at it critically. Econo-egocentrism is, like any worldview, so complex, interrelated, and pervasive that it is difficult to examine. However, all its values, beliefs, and connections stem from one fundamental understanding about the source of human worth. Econo-egocentrism depends on the understanding that human worth is extrinsic. The extrinsic worth philosophy holds that worth is not something we have inherently, as an immutable part of our being, but is something we have to earn. We are thus led to believe that we are of worth only if we gain whatever we feel can give us worth. We must *have* certain material possessions or qualities, *have* knowledge that is considered valuable, or *have* skills to perform certain tasks that are deemed important by the society.

We feel that if we are to have any significance in the eyes of others and in our own eyes, we are going to have to earn it. Worth, we think, doesn't come naturally. If we want to "be somebody," we have to do it ourselves.

The fear of never making it, of never finding significance drives us to earn, gain, acquire, win, succeed, develop, conquer, achieve, secure, in order to prove that we "have what it takes" to "become somebody." We become "somebody" if we *have* one or more attributes such as good looks, money, brains, athletic ability, nice personality, political power, sex appeal, religion, health, education, popularity, new car, nice home, smart children, good job, the right contacts.

What we think we must *have* is different for different sectors of the society. For some it is a Cadillac, while for others a pick-up truck is most highly valued. For some it is the job you have, for others it is how much money you make and the job itself is irrelevant. Earning a Ph.D., making touchdowns, wearing fashionable clothes, owning valuable real estate, or sleeping with the most people are deemed to be significant and offer various degrees of worth for various people.

Sometimes what we consider the basis of our worth is very valuable in and of itself. We may feel we are of worth because we teach well, counsel or heal others, bring beauty into the world through art, or because we are loved. These make us feel good and are beneficial for society. However, they can also be seen as the source of our worth. If we were unable to be involved in such activities or lost the love of others we would believe we were less significant. Often these things come to be important for us not only for their own sake, but also for the worth we feel we gain from them.

People become identified, to themselves as well as to others, by what they have earned, what they know, and what they can do. A "doctor" is not a person but a role. The "doctor" is deemed to have worth because he or she knows certain things and can do certain things. A "garbage collector" is also not a person but a role. However, because much more knowledge is required for a person to act as a doctor than to act as a garbage collector, the extrinsic worth philosophy dictates that the person who has the role of collecting garbage is of less worth in our culture than the physician.

This shows up dramatically in the comparison of the money that each role brings to the persons who fill those roles, even though doctors and garbage collectors are both engaged in the same general effort of keeping the citizenry heathy. It is ironic to note that should all the doctors and garbage collectors go on strike, the general populace would miss the garbage collectors sooner than they would miss the doctors.

The standards by which people must measure themselves are determined by the group with which they identify. This is, of course, a matter of different tastes and experiences, but the basic perspective remains the same: the only way we think we can be of worth is to *have* whatever it is we deem significant.

This extrinsic worth understanding of what gives significance and meaning to life has a formula that we hear from the day we are born to the day we die. It is simple: If you have ______, then you will ______. "If you have the right attitude, you will have success." "If you have what it takes, you will get what you want." "If you have the right religion, you will be saved."

The *having* formula has other forms, but they all give the same message about extrinsic worth. "If you will use our toothpaste, you will have a sexy smile." "If you study hard, you will surpass the others." "If you practice, you will win." Sometimes the formula is put in the negative: "If you don't rock the boat, you will get ahead." "If you don't live up to my expectations, I won't love you." Various forms of this latter statement, verbalized or not, can play havoc with a person's life by causing guilt, conformity, and suppressed self-expression.

If/then sequences can be valuable ways of understanding our environment: If I put my hand in the fire, I will get burned. But when used in terms of gaining worth they are not so useful. "If you practice, then you will win" might indeed be true. But it just as easily might not.

Fearing Loss and Falling Short

> *I am afraid to tell you who I am, because, if I tell you who I am, you may not like who I am, and it's all that I have.*
>
> —John Powell

One problem with the extrinsic worth philosophy is that what can be gained can also be lost. Possessions can be destroyed, knowledge surpassed, and skills outmoded. The glory of achievements can fade with time. If our significance is tied to something that we can lose or can be taken away from us, then the base we have built for our self-esteem is shaky. Therefore we sense that we must continually be on watch to protect our significance.

Since we always run the risk of losing extrinsic worth, we feel we must gain as much worth as possible. We think that the more we have the less we will suffer if we lose some. We feel we must consume the latest in technology, rise further in the organization, win the championship again, somehow do more or better than before.

Only by continually trying to *have* more can we feel somewhat assured that our worth is safe.

Psychoanalyst Erich Fromm asks, *"If I am what I have and if what I have is lost, who then am I?...* Because I *can* lose what I have, I am necessarily constantly worried that I *shall* lose what I have." He says that this makes us fear love, freedom, growth, change, and the unknown. We "become defensive, hard, suspicious, lonely, driven by the need to have more in order to be better protected."[1]

Fear is the root of many other emotions and behaviors. When we act angry, hateful, or apathetic, quite often what we are really feeling is fear. Though it may not be recognized, the fear of losing the bit of worth we have struggled for affects us deeply. It can thus elicit very strong reactions. If we feel our worth is threatened we may become hostile and domineering or self-loathing and submissive. As in any threatening situation our instinctive responses are either fight or flight. The fear of losing our worth may cause us to strike back in anger or hatred, or to act as a "bully" or "expert," protecting ourselves by trying to control the situation. This fear can also cause us to avoid expressing ourselves, standing up for our ideas, or trying new situations where we might risk being wrong or appearing foolish. We build fortresses to protect ourselves and discover that we have built prisons.

A second problem with the theory of extrinsic worth is that there is no set point at which we become "of worth." Thus we are never sure if now, finally, we are of *enough* worth or if we're still not quite there. Not being secure in our worth we continue to feel inadequate and continue to search, struggle, or scavenge for significance.

This sense of inadequacy may come from feeling that we have failed those we look up to, persons who are important influences in our lives because of either respect or fear. What we perceive as the expectations of these others often become our expectations of ourselves. The voices of authority figures heard when we were young often stay with us throughout life. This socialization process establishes the need in our minds for attaining extrinsic worth. As a result, we may spend our lives with some of these authority figures, in a sense, "looking over our shoulder." No matter how hard some people try, they find they can never please these "ghosts" of the past who continually remind them to do better.

This feeling of having let someone down leads to the unfocused sense of guilt that afflicts so many millions of people. Sometimes, the word "God" is used to name these "ghosts," which not only makes the guilt more burdensome, but also produces a theology devoid of joy and celebration. Only when we perceive we have done something to prove our worth and significance can we feel we have lived up to someone's expectations.

Digging Holes

> *Some of us often feel, and most of us sometimes feel, that we are only someone if we have "made it" and can look down on whose who have not.*
>
> —Robert Bellah et al.

Because there is no exact measurement of when we are of worth and when we are not, personal significance is relative to the perceived significance of others. Thus there is a constant comparing of one's position with the position of peers and members of reference groups. It is a matter of staying ahead of the Joneses, or at least keeping up with them. It is a matter of keeping an eye on who got promoted, who has the latest state-of-the-art technology, who is getting more dates, which player has the best average, whose car will accelerate from zero to sixty faster so that we know the nature of our competition.

This comparing may lead us to feel that by looking down on others we gain a bit of worth. We can get a psychological boost from thinking that someone else is more of a failure, or less educated, or automatically of less significance because of their skin color or sex or religion. We may not be the best, "...but *at least* we're better than they are!"

Olive Schreiner tells a story about dreaming that God took her on a tour of Hell. While there, she saw people digging holes and covering them up so no one else could see them. She asked God what these people were doing. God replied that the holes were for others to fall into. "Why?" the dreamer asked. God replied that these people thought that when others fell into the holes the diggers would gain significance because they were now higher than those who had fallen. "Are these people sane?" asked the dreamer. God replied, "There are no sane people in Hell."[2]

In our attempt to feel "better than" and therefore to have more significance than others, we go around "digging holes" into which others may fall. We are alert for situations in which we can look down on others. Many times we use teasing or kidding. Even "good natured" kidding reveals the awkwardness we feel in relating to another person without trying to lower the other person in some way. Sometimes we use "putdowns" or taunting or sarcasm. We can observe the media and life all around us and note how much of what we call humor is the result of someone falling into a "hole." We start rumors and spread gossip and, often without realizing it, wait for chances to prove we are better than someone else.

Such hierarchical, "ladder" mentality leads us to be obsessed with "ranking." We keep a close eye on the constant jockeying of the top forty songs, the week-by-week shifts in the TV ratings, and the top ten of any category imaginable, because it matters so much to us who is "higher" than whom. Team rankings, Fortune 500, the *New York Times* Best Seller list—we must know who is higher and therefore better. Comparison and ladder climbing seem to be the only ways we know how to determine what is of value and what is not.

This approach is learned early in life and we have all experienced it many times. It has been referred to as the basic game that people play. "Mine Is Better Than Yours." You may have heard that phrase sung by children teasing others. The words vary but the tune is always mockingly the same adaptation of "Ring Around the Rosie."

Digging holes works both ways, for we are not the only diggers. Each of us has, more than likely, felt that we have fallen into many holes that have been dug for us so that others might feel superior. When we lose, when someone gloats over their ability to do something better, when we are immediately treated as second-class citizens because of being black, or old, or handicapped, or overweight—in such situations we feel we have fallen into a hole. Those who put us down feel they suddenly have more worth than we do and, looking up at them from where we have been knocked into the dirt, we feel they might be right.

In such a situation we may accept that they are "better" and continue to look up to them. In looking up to others we wish to have as much significance as they. This causes us to think as they do, or to dress, buy, vote, play, talk, as they do. Hero worship develops from persons feeling they can gain some amount of significance by associating themselves, however distantly, with the famous. There are some who even associate themselves through religion to the word "God" and gain a feeling of superiority over those who are less fortunate in their associations.

The other reaction to falling in a hole is quickly to dig a deeper hole in hopes that someone else might fall in. We would still be in a hole, of course, but we would then be of some worth, we tell ourselves, because there would be someone who seems lower than we are.

Often without realizing it, we come to treat some people worse than we treat others just because they don't meet certain standards of significance that we feel are important. We may not treat a streetperson as we would the vice-president of a bank. And we may not feel that a high-school dropout has as much significance as a someone with a Ph.D. Or, as is sometimes the case, we may feel that the person who owns a Porsche deserves less respect than someone who drives an old Ford because the Porsche driver is trying to appear better than we are. The word "enemy" is a hole into which we throw those we fear so we don't have to "respect" them as equals. Usually, when others call us "enemy," we accept the designation and start digging a hole for them. Many people, wanting to prove something about themselves, go looking for enemies. They always find them.

We invent labels to categorize people into groups so we can distinguish who is of worth and who is not. If someone is labeled a "communist," some of us immediately feel that person is not of worth. To others, a "capitalist" is similarly lacking in significance. If you are black, Oriental, white, Native American, young, old, rich, poor, male, female, you are immediately less significant. We fall into this attitude of "isms" (racism, ageism, sexism, classism) because we want to classify others into relative levels of worth so we have an idea of how our own sense of worth compares. If we can designate a large segment of the population as insignificant, then we have dug a hole for them and we feel our worth increased.

The struggle for a sense of worth engenders rivalry between those who might otherwise be friends. It can cause jealousy when one seems to "have more" things, knowledge, or skills than another. The never-ending need for proving one's worth in one way or another leads to greed. If this need is not satisfied, which it can never be, frustration or anger results. Success, however temporary, tends to produce pride. Failure begets guilt.

Grasping at Straws

> *According to the Teachers, there is only one thing that all people possess equally. This is their loneliness. No two people on the face of the earth are alike in any one thing except for their loneliness. This is the cause of our growing, but it is also the cause of our wars. Love, hate, greed and generosity are all rooted within our loneliness, within our desire to be needed and loved.*
>
> — Hyemeyohsts Storm

Trying to attain worth seems to be such a fruitless, frustrating, harmful venture. Why do we continue in its painful path? Simply because we believe that there is no other way. Since we feel we have no inherent worth, the search for meaning and significance becomes the driving force in our lives. Feeling empty and insignificant, fearing our ultimate meaninglessness, we find our most pressing need is to discover or gain or earn some feeling of worth in what seems to be a huge and unconcerned universe.

It is this sort of angst and alienation that many philosophers, theologians, artists, and others feel has characterized Western life in the twentieth century. Such a feeling of meaninglessness causes us to grasp at a variety of experiences that we feel might give our lives significance. Attributing such vital importance to basic activities or possessions leads to the abundance of addictions and obsessions we find in our society. Alcohol and other drugs, competition, sexual performance, body-building, dieting, job status, political influence, and material possessions can all be used to escape from our feelings of not having enough significance in our own estimation or the estimation of others.

We rarely think of consuming as an addiction, but the search for meaning through material goods is obvious in our society. Just as an alcoholic turns to drink when depressed, upset, or frustrated, many of us try to make ourselves feel better through buying something. We have been socialized to think that buying and owning are very significant activities. Through participating in these "significant" acts we hope to experience significance in our lives.

Any addiction or obsession promises significance and escape

from worthlessness — either through numbing our minds to the situation (drugs, alcohol, TV) or through attaining a certain standard of worth (becoming thin, winning, owning more things). Feeling empty and insignificant, we run to these things in hopes they will fill the void for us.

The social institution that could, and should, serve to alleviate such a sense of meaningless alienation has itself succumbed to the idea of extrinsic worth. Church people talk about being called to be "in, but not of," the world. This should mean offering an alternative to societal values, goals, and behaviors, but this has all too frequently not been the case (see chap. 11).

Not only have the churches failed to offer a substantive alternative, they have to a large extent promoted the idea of extrinsic worth. The version of extrinsic worth found in popular theology is that we are sinners and we must earn salvation. Advocates of this view also claim that there is a Hell, a place for those who do not meet certain conditions. They seem to believe, paradoxically, that God's love is unconditional, but only in certain circumstances. Just as they think our worldly worth is conditional, they also think that God's love has requirements.

Many church people are believers in the having formula. They are conditioned by the idea of extrinsic worth to think in terms of having. By having they come to feel that they are significant, and this spills over easily into their religious thinking. People talk much about having faith, having salvation, having a relationship with God, having a fine church building or a magnificent religious TV program. There is always talk about having numerous members and having more programs than other groups, having a fine priest or preacher, having an active youth program, having a new parking lot. There seems to be the feeling that these things determine which congregation is more significant and who is worthy of God's love.

Thus except in the ever-present, though overwhelmed, first tradition, there is no strong opposition to the philosophy of extrinsic worth. With no opposition, no projected alternatives, it is not surprising that the idea of extrinsic worth has gained such loyalty and credibility. It thus remains the firm foundation for econoegocentrism and our society.

See below chapter 14, "Trying It on for Size," pages 133ff., nos. 20, 22, 30, and 31.

See below chapter 15, "Food for Thought," pages 168ff., nos. 6, 28, 33, and 43.

CHAPTER 4

Our Dominant Worldview...

Even Adam Smith, perhaps the person most directly responsible for the materialistic and economic nature of modern civilization, clearly believed that a man who pursued wealth was prey to vanity, greed, and other foolish and ignoble motives. —William Ophuls

The philosophy of extrinsic worth has shaped our ideas and attitudes in all areas of our daily lives. Like the bedrock under our feet, the ethic of extrinsic worth underlies our worldview and determines the form of our society. Understanding the importance and role of this idea can illuminate econo-egocentrism and why our society is the way it is.

The idea of extrinsic worth deftly penetrates and controls much of our lives by determining the perspective we have on life and the ways we relate to others. Since we feel that we are not of worth unless we earn it, it becomes of vital importance to find, earn, win any significance we can. Thus the search and struggle for extrinsic worth becomes the driving force, the determining factor, the primary activity for much of our lives. It influences our decisions, helps determine our goals, and causes us to act in certain ways. The need for extrinsic worth often becomes the major factor in a career choice, the use of money, the development of relationships, and our own sense of well-being and esteem.

Belief in extrinsic worth is a pervasive cultural trait. As the driving force for the vast majority of Americans, it is an important factor in the way our society works. Or doesn't work. If we are sensitive to the struggle for extrinsic worth as a motivating factor throughout the society we begin to realize that it is at the root of many of our societal woes—from rape to insider trading scandals, from drug abuse to unemployment, from mis-education to a lack of voter turnout.

It may seem farfetched that one factor can underlie so many problems, or that one idea can so influence an entire society. But this fundamental idea determines our very understanding of who we are. Realizing that this overwhelming spectrum of problems is actually part of the same basic problem can make the situation seem less intimidating, confusing, and hopeless. As when trying to save a tree from a vast entanglement of vines, we find our task is much easier if all the vines grow from the same stem. We may find that we can tackle our problems more effectively at the source than at each branch and tendril.

Being aware of extrinsic worth as a determining factor in our lives and relationships can also help explain actions and attitudes that are otherwise enigmatic. Even though our intentions are "good" and we feel we are kind, moral, honest folk, we still "do what we wouldn't and don't do what we would."

Why do we act this way? Why do we get ourselves into ways of relating to others that are not healthy and mutually enhancing? Why do "good" people do "bad" things? These sorts of questions often confound us, and, unanswered, they hamper any attempts to act, or expect others to act, differently. Without understanding the cause or motive of such behavior we find it difficult to change it. Understanding the need for extrinsic worth clarifies the motivation of such actions. Convinced that we must gain extrinsic worth, we will try almost anything to do so. The need for worth cannot be held in check. It can induce us to act in ways we otherwise would not.

Because our worldview teaches us that the search for worth is the most important need in our lives, we tend to focus on that need. This means focusing on ourselves. The idea of extrinsic worth causes us to develop a frame of reference that is markedly egocentric.

Egocentrism

> *In our egocentricity the world revolves about us as a shadowy existence whence people and things are called forth according to our wants, then permitted to recede into their indefinite background.*
>
> —Conrad Bonifazi

Egocentrism, as its name suggests, means being self-focused. Attention and interest are constantly focused on the self. All acts. endeavors, and relationships have as their primary purpose enhancing or protecting the self in some way, and thereby gaining, or hanging on to, a sense of worth. This is not to say that egocentrism necessarily implies egoism. Egocentric persons, unlike the egoistic ones, do not necessarily feel that they are better than other people. Instead, egocentric persons more often feel that they are not as good as others and thus must constantly be aiding and protecting themselves. The self seems empty and fragile and, in order to survive, it must be constantly attended.

Because our worldview encourages us to be self-focused, it is difficult for us to be open to others, to understand their needs and joys, to even "see" them clearly. Egocentrism is like looking into a convex mirror or the back of a spoon. The curve distorts the view so that one's nose is huge and the rest of one's face is small in comparison. Egocentrism similarly distorts our perspective so that we ourselves seem much larger than everything else around us. Since our own needs are seen and felt to be more important than the needs of others, interaction with others tends to be self-serving. Instead of being mutually enhancing and supporting and valued for its own sake, a relationship based on egocentrism is often only valued because it gives us a sense of worth in some way.

Participants in such a relationship fall into the trap of either feeling dependent or independent. Though usually seen as contradictory, independence and dependence are actually sides of the same egocentric coin. Both are self-focused and manipulative; both perceive relationships as means of gaining worth.

If we feel dependent on another, we avoid competition and do not have to make decisions or take responsibility for our actions. This protects our worth from possible risks. We also feel we gain worth by identification with the reference person or group on which we feel dependent and to which we attribute worth.

Independence is also egocentric, for it includes the refusal to admit need of anyone else. If we do not need anyone else we feel free to focus totally on ourselves. When we pride ourselves on our independence we see anyone we are connected with as dependent upon us. We feel we gain worth from this for we feel more powerful, more intelligent, and generally better than the other. (The fact that we are dependent on the other in order to feel powerful goes unrealized or denied.)

Egocentrism is a self-perpetuating cycle: the more we focus on ourselves the less we know about others. The less we know, the less we care and the more we focus on ourselves. The effects of this cycle are frightening when we consider that few children in American schools learn much about the history, geography, or cultures of the rest of the world. If self-focused ignorance leads to apathy, how does this affect our international relations? What we call egocentrism at the individual level becomes nationalism when it concerns the entire country.

Viewing the world through an egocentric frame of reference means that everything we do or hope to do is important only if we feel we gain from it. How it affects others is eclipsed by how it affects us. It is important to re-emphasize that being self-focused does not necessarily mean we feel superior to others. This may be the case, but more precisely it refers to the inability to look beyond ourselves and empathize with others.

Egocentrism blocks us from opening up to and thus reaching out to others. The search for worth can be so all-consuming that we have no time or energy to move beyond ourselves. Even worse, it can impel us to cause pain and suffering for others. In fact, at times we may feel that if others suffer from our actions we may look good in comparison to them. In this way we "dig holes" for others.

Such mental processes enable us to be spiteful, unfriendly, and insensitive in many ways. If we feel our worth is threatened, we strike out to protect it, either physically or with teasing, insults, or any multitude of "socially acceptable" ways of making another feel uncomfortable or hurt. At times we think that we are doing something kind when we are actually digging holes by "putting someone in their place" or "doing it for their own good." At other times we may know we are acting insensitively, but can't seem to avoid it. We don't do this because we are cruel people. We are motivated to act this way, usually against our conscious wishes and often to our own surprise, because our need to protect our worth is so strong. Our egocentric perspective leads us to feel that our own needs and feelings are more important than others'.

Violence and crime are the extreme results of this egocentric insensitivity. We become so focused on our anger or grievance that we either don't realize or don't care how the other person will be affected. Our need for worth is so strong that it overcomes our human sentiments and outweighs another person's needs, well-being, or even another's life.

Child abuse is conceivable only when an adult feels the need for control and power is more important than the child's need for health and nurturing. Rape can be committed only when a man believes that his need for dominance obliterates any concern for a woman's physical and mental well-being. Murder is deemed possible only if someone feels his anger or wounded honor is more important than another person's life.

Since economic gain is believed to be a major source of worth in econo-egocentrism, it is not surprising that we often act as though profit is more important than people. This distortion of priorities can be used to justify harming others for the sake of personal, monetary gain. This attitude can be seen readily in armed robbery, kidnapping, extortion. We see the injustice in these acts and label them "crimes."

The same attitude, however, enables many other unjust acts that are not labelled "crimes" because they are more socially accepted. We place profits over people when we refuse to allow a shelter for the homeless to be built near our home or business because we fear it will decrease property value. We invest in companies with questionable policies or products because it's a "good" business. Industries create products that are harmful or of poor quality and often mislead consumers through advertising.

Such profits-over-people policies are especially frightening when they involve food, medicine, or technology such as nuclear power. Because the first tradition of values still has some effect on us, we have established watchdog groups to hold these practices in check. Such citizen groups are necessary because of our societal egocentrism. If it were not for this egocentric attitude, regulations and guidelines would rarely be necessary.

The desire for extrinsic worth and an egocentric frame of reference cause us to relate to others in certain ways. The two primary ways of relating in our econo-egocentric society are competition and conformity.

Competition

> *Trying to be number one in all situations may be rooted in self-esteem needs, but it can be driven by the force of habit as well. We simply become accustomed to thinking along these lines.* —Alfie Kohn

Competition is activity in which a person or a group seeks to achieve a goal faster, better than, or to the exclusion of another person or group. In competition there is only one winner; all the rest of the strivers become losers. Competition undermines any sense of community because the joy of winning is always at the expense of those who lose. Even the camaraderie between teammates or business partners is weakened through competition for honors and promotions. Everyone who competes is interested in winning because victory gives a sense of having gained significance.

Competition pervades almost every aspect of our lives, from romance to industry, from recreation to international relations. In whatever we are doing we are urged to win, to beat out the other guy, to prove our superiority. To be a good fighter is expected. To win, to be "Number 1," is the highest goal.

Much of our devotion to competition is based on two myths. The first is that aggressive competition is part of human nature. We often claim that it is a natural instinct to compete and feel aggression toward others. This belief is quite widespread even though there is no conclusive evidence to support it.

What has emerged in studies of various groups is that human beings are capable of learning almost any kind of lifestyle. There are no genes for hate and aggression and no genes for love and compassion. Humans are capable of learning either one or the other or both. "Either of these capacities—for love or for hate—can be reinforced in such a way that it begets a more dominant set of values and behavior patterns than the other."[1]

The Hopi, for example, were a very peaceful and internally cooperative tribe living in the midst of other tribes who stressed warfare and competition. Cooperative, communal groups have likewise existed in our extremely competitive society since its very beginnings. It cannot be said, therefore, that competition is an inevitable part of human nature. What we can say at most is that competition is one possible cultural form in many parts of the world and certainly is dominant in the United States.

The second myth supporting the idea of competition is that we need the motivation of competition in order to feel we've done something important. We feel we must compete in order to "do our best," overcome our limitations, or try something new. We think we need the incentive of winning, and the fear of losing, in order to strive for a goal. Even if we are not competing with others we feel the need to "beat our own record" in order to feel we've done something important.

We have the idea that there are two kinds of competition: "neurotic" competition, in which the need to win is taken to an extreme, and "healthy" competition, which challenges, motivates, and advances us. But there is no qualitative difference between the two; there is merely a difference in degree. It becomes very difficult to draw a line between them and therefore very easy to extend "social acceptability" to competition that is obviously "neurotic" and harmful.

The opinion that competition is necessary to motivate us is a cynical view that fails to take into account the human sentiments of love and compassion, curiosity and creativity. Have we truly accomplished more of value because of competition? Or is it human nature to try new things, to invent ways to make life easier or just to see if something can be done? The first time someone purposely planted a seed, some 8,000 years ago, it is doubtful that she did so through a competitive urge—to be the first to invent agriculture or to prove that Mesopotamia was Number 1. More likely she did it to see what would happen, to see if maybe this might provide more food for her children.

Without competition we would still invent, create, strive, and dream. Young children accomplish amazing things in the first few years of life without competing at all. This natural creativity and curiosity stays with us throughout life—if we allow it expression. We do not need competition; we couldn't stop being creative if we wanted to.

Regardless of how we rationalize and sacralize our obsession with competition, the reason we compete is because we think we can gain worth by doing so. In our society, winning is highly valued and is thus believed to be a source of worth. If I am Number 1, I feel assured that, since I am better than everyone else, I must have worth. So highly do we value competition that even if we lose we can comfort ourselves by saying "at least we tried." Those who compete, even the "losers," are accorded more worth than those who "don't even try."

Competition is reinforced by the esteem given to those who have competed well. Winners (whether they be from sports, politics, the Top 40 chart, or the Emmy awards) have fame, popularity, money, power. To be Number 1 is *really* to be of worth; Number 2 just doesn't cut it: there's still someone with more worth. We are socialized to believe that being a winner assures significance.

What we don't see is how, out of the limelight and off camera, "winners" begin to feel frustrated and dissatisfied. They don't feel quite significant enough; they aren't so sure they have worth anymore. It is once again the problem that what can be gained can also be lost. When someone else beats your record or wins your position, your worth suddenly diminishes.

Competition can be addictive. Winning once is just not enough. After a while we have to win again and then again in order to feel we are still of worth. The worth we feel we gain through competition fades quickly. We must continue to compete in order to retain a sense of worth and to ensure that no one surpasses us. If our significance is relative to those around us, we can never stop competing. While we rest, others might move past us, overshadowing and devaluing all that we struggled to acquire.

Conformity

> *The fear of our feelings is not the only one that inhibits the creative process. The fear of being stupid is the most pervasive, and the fear of failure is the most powerful of all. Both stem from another, more basic fear: that of rejection.* —Lois Robbins

The other basic approach we have for relating to each other in an econo-egocentric society is conformity, that is, the process of patterning our behavior, appearance, or attitude on some external standard.

Some conformity is necessary in society. There is a basic socialization process we all go through as we grow up that teaches us how to behave in our culture. We learn to shake hands when meeting someone, to knock before entering someone's house, and not to spit in church. This is the conformity that is natural in a society and varies from culture to culture. Another form of necessary conformity is responsible behavior. We conform when we stop at a stop sign, throw our garbage in trashcans instead of on the street, and move out of the way of ambulances. Such conforming behavior prevents chaos and enables the society to function.

Such conformity is necessary and inevitable. Conformity, however, can be taken to an extreme in which one's own feelings, preferences, and beliefs are lost or rejected in favor of some external standard. The external standard may be a certain principle or idealized goal; it may be a reference person or group, the opinion of an "expert," or the evanescent declarations of "fashion"; it may be a circumstance that pushes us to accept that "everyone is doing it," or "when in Rome, do as the Romans do." We conform because we want to be accepted, because we want to be associated with a certain group, and because we fear being laughed at, being looked down on, or being wrong. We conform because we think it is a way to attain, or at least protect, worth.

It may seem odd that a society so obsessed with competition should also value conformity. Yet these two behaviors are complementary and reinforce each other in many ways. Where there is a constant push for competition, there can be little sense of community. If there is little sense of community, people feel alienated and try various means to overcome their alienation. Conformity is one way of doing this, for it makes the social situation look like community even though it is not. Competition divides people, but people need each other. The simplest way of trying to be part of a group is to conform.

Since competition is so valued in our society we are expected to compete. We therefore conform to the norm of competition. Often trying to be the most "in" person of a group, we compete to see who can conform the most fully.

Observers of our culture as far back as the time of Andrew Jackson saw that despite the stress on individualism and self-centered activities, Americans did not feel as free and uninhibited as they liked to think. Alexis de Tocqueville noted, "I know no country in which there is so little true independence of mind and freedom of discussion as in America."[2] Harriet Martineau wrote, "The worship of Opinion is, at this day, the established religion of the United States."[3]

In the United States, especially in the early days, one was expected to conform to the idea that this country was the great hope of the world, for it was founded on the principle of individual liberty. Anyone who had doubts about the excesses of individual liberty was in the strange predicament of feeling pressured not to express those doubts. The norm of conformity was too strong. Throughout our history, community and free expression have been continually undercut by the pressure to conform.

Those who banded together in communal groups were wondered about and even considered deviant. The labor union movement was hampered for years by workers conforming to the cultural tradition of individualism. Today people think they are expressing their individualism by consuming in distinctive, personal ways. It is not realized that consuming, in whatever style, is conforming to the cultural norm that defines reality in terms of the market place.

When we think of conformity in American society we think immediately of people using drugs or following the latest fads. But this is just a very obvious example of a phenomenon pervasive in American society. We conform in our families ("No child of mine will ever...," "Why can't you be like your sister?"). We conform in politics ("The polls say this guy is way behind. I'm not going to vote for him if no one else is. I don't want to waste my vote." "This is a partisan issue—you'd better toe the party line."). We conform in business and industry ("If other factories have evaded the pollution regulations we can too"; "Don't rock the boat and you'll move up the ladder."). And we conform most often in our role as consumer ("They say this is what everyone will be wearing this fall." "All the kids have transformers! I want one, too!"). Kids are not the only ones to use the claim that "everybody's doing it" to increase the appeal and justify the rightness of any action.

Conforming is important in our relating to others because we see it as a major way to gain and protect our worth. We allow society or the subgroup with which we identify to determine what gives worth. Therefore we feel we must conform to these standards or else we will not be seen as significant. If my reference group defines worth in terms of a graduate degree and a good income, I will feel I have less worth if I don't finish school or am unemployed.

Another way that conforming gives us worth is through associating with those we feel have worth. We look up to these persons because we feel they have earned worth and significance. We think that by being like them we, too, may have worth. This is part of the reason Americans love "stars." A "star" is, to the fans, clearly of worth and significance. We dress, act, and share opinions of those we look up to, whether they are famous or just the most popular people in the school, in hopes of gaining significance through association.

We conform so we do not seem unworthy in the eyes of those we admire. This can lead us to reject and disparage our own opinions, values, tastes, and interests, thus belittling our identity. It can also cause us to act against our sense of what is appropriate and against our better judgment. How many times have we done something we regretted later just because we wanted to be socially accepted?

With an egocentric frame of reference, competition and conformity are the most logical and the most obvious ways of relating to other people. They may also be the only ones, for there are limited ways we can relate while still focusing on ourselves. This does not mean, however, that our egocentric frame of reference is limited to those actions we readily see as competing or conforming. Competition and conformity are not confined to football games and fashion trends, corporate takeovers and keeping up with the Joneses. There are many attitudes and ways of thinking and acting that begin to become second nature when competition and conformity are the only ways of relating. These expressions of our worldview reinforce our egocentric frame of reference and are useful tools in the search for extrinsic worth.

See chapter 14 below, "Trying It on for Size," pages 133ff., nos. 7, 18, and 19.

See chapter 15 below, "Food for Thought," pages 168ff., nos. 34, 37, and 40.

CHAPTER 5

. . . And How It's Expressed

My own behavior baffles me. . . . I often find that I have the will to do good, but not the power. That is, I don't accomplish the good I set out to do, and the evil I don't really want to do I find I am always doing.
—Romans 7:15–19 (Phillips)

We have been using "econo-egocentrism" as a noun, an entity. It is important to realize, however, that this worldview, or any worldview, is not a *thing;* it is merely a *concept* that is used to try to describe people treating people in certain ways. Econo-egocentrism is a concept that points to much more than people being egocentric, competitive, and conformist. These are the primary manifestations of the worldview, but they combine and interact to influence how we think and act in many different ways.

Dualistic Thinking

If one were to devise a way in which to best kill creativity, one would be hard put to invent anything more surely effective than to instruct persons in dualistic thinking and dualistic feeling and dualistic living. The problem with this is that it kills God, it kills the spirit, it kills the human person who cannot live humanly without creativity.
—Matthew Fox

Dualistic thinking is a perspective on reality in which everything is seen as split into opposing extremes: black/white, right/wrong, good/evil. Thus, there is only one right way of doing or being. Any variance from this way must be wrong. Dualistic thinking is rooted deeply in the consciousness of our culture. The mythical framework of all Indo-European peoples is based on a fundamental struggle between the forces of good and those of evil. This dualism is often expressed in Western imagery as God and Satan. We all know the images: good guys always wear white, the young prince must defeat the evil sorcerer. The battle between good and evil is seen as the basic struggle in the world, or in the cosmos according to ancient myths and current science fiction fantasies. This mythic structure continues to determine how we think and how we understand our differences.

We are so influenced by these images that a U.S. president referred to the Soviet Union as "the Evil Empire." Because the Soviets differ from us ideologically, we see them as "the bad guys," and as a threat to our "good" way of life. The Soviets, of course, see the situation in reverse. Thus, Americans fear the Soviet economic system, their supposed "communism," and in turn the Soviets vilify and denounce the evils of capitalism.

Since anything that is not good must be bad, dualistic thinking has no room for in-betweens, maybes, or creative alternatives. It allows no concept of variation or possibilities that do not fit the polarized view of the situation. Thus dualistic thinking enforces conformity by demanding that everything must be on one side or the other. If a nation is not on "our side" it *must* be aligned with the Soviets. If you are against busing you *must* be a racist. Like in a giant true/false quiz we are locked into two possibilities, not allowing ourselves or others to take alternative positions or even realizing that such choices exist.

Competition is dependent on dualistic thinking, for we must have the ability to see others as totally separate from ourselves before we can compete with them. In order to compete we must have something to strive against. Competition depends on the differentiation between me and you, us and them, this way and that way. We must feel that our differences place us on distinct sides before we can compete with each other.

Dualistic thinking is an ingenious construction for attempting to gain worth because it insures that we will "win." By dividing between "us" and "them" we feel we immediately gain worth because at least we are not one of "them." We feel we gain even more worth when we label "them" as "bad" and "us" as "good." That way we not only feel we have worth because we are "good," but we also protect ourselves from the risk of losing any worth. Even if the "good guys" lose, they feel they still gain worth because they "fought the good fight."

Exclusionist Attitude

> *Those who could not bear to have beggars, former prostitutes, servants, women and children treated as their equals, who could not live without feeling superior to at least some people, would simply not be at home in God's kingdom as Jesus understood it. They would want to exclude themselves from it.*
>
> —Albert Nolan

Dualistic thinking elicits an attitude of exclusionism, a feeling that it is legitimate for some people to "lose out." In this way of thinking it is logical to assume that, because some people are "right" and others are "wrong," those who are "right" deserve to be better off. Those who are "haves" deserve to be "haves"; therefore, those who have nothing must deserve nothing.

We like to feel that it is okay for some to be excluded from success. If everyone were successful, success would not mean as much. We suffer from an idea left over from the Puritan ethic that holds that those who succeed are favored by God and those who do not succeed are being punished for their sins. By the rationalization that we deserve all we have, the exclusionist attitude also helps assuage any guilt we might feel concerning poverty, hunger, and an unequal distribution of wealth.

The exclusionist attitude elicits a sense that those who are not like us are not as good as we are. Whether the difference is economic, cultural, racial, or in physical appearance or ability, we have the idea that it somehow denotes inferiority. It is this attitude that has caused minorities to have to struggle for the civil rights that go without question to those in power. From an academic distance many have frowned on caste Hindus because they have traditionally identified themselves as being "better." But even in America, the land of supposed equality and justice, blacks and Native Americans have been deemed nonhuman and without souls, and signs saying "No Jews Allowed" or "No Irish Need Apply" used to be commonplace. Today we have affirmative action and anti-discrimination laws, but such laws wouldn't be necessary without the impact of the exclusionist attitude.

Someone must be the loser so we know we are the winners. Even if we are not exactly winners we can deem ourselves important because we are not as bad off as someone else. People who never feel they catch up with the Joneses can comfort themselves with the thought that *at least* they are better off than the Culleys.

Directive Power

Power over, domination and control, feed best on deprecations of the human, hardly on granting him his esteem and value. —Joseph Chilton Pearce

Another important facet of econo-egocentrism is directive *power.* This is "the capacity of an individual to increase his satisfactions by intentionally . . . shaping and using the behavior of others to advance his interests." It is based on the ability to force others to enhance oneself with no thought of the common good. Directive power is using our power, physically or psychologically, to make others do what we want.[1]

Directive power is usually what we are referring to when we talk of "power" in the social, economic, and political sense. The "powerful" people in a society are those who can force others, through a variety of subtle and direct means, to do as they wish. They are the rich and the famous, the corporation presidents, and the influential politicians. They are also persons who "lead" cliques or who manipulate whatever committees they are on. Since those who are seen to be "powerful" are often those understood to be the most significant, it becomes socially acceptable and admirable to use directive power. Because violence is a form of directive power, it also gains a degree of social acceptability, as can be seen in cop shows, westerns, war toys, and the monuments we erect to honor warriors.

It seems a basic idea to us: the more power I have, the more I can influence the situation to suit my interests. We rarely, if ever, consider that "power" can be used for the benefit of all, as in the cases of Gandhi and Martin Luther King, Jr. We will return to this alternative form of power in chapter 8.

Directive power can be a great source of extrinsic worth. We feel very important and worthy when we can make others do what we want. If we have the power to dominate in this way we feel we must have more worth than others.

Directive power is also a way of competing. If I can make you do what I want, I win. Directive power stimulates, and is aided by, conformity because those who wield the power enforce conformity to their will. Others conform in hopes that they will gain worth through association. Directive power is manifest through competition by those who have power and through conformity by those who do not.

Expertism

If by distortion and tricks the public is manipulated into seeming to make its own choices without actually doing so, it is not free. —Daniel Yankelovich

Conforming to the opinions of those in power or authority is called expertism. Those who claim to be "experts" are always right, we believe, and we doubt our own knowledge or feelings if they contradict those of the experts. As a result, we entrust the experts with the right to make important decisions concerning our lives.

Expertism fits our egocentric need by suggesting worth can be gained through agreement with those who, because they are experts, must have worth. It also insures that we won't risk our sense of worth by being wrong. Expertism also tends to cause the experts to feel they are worth more than other people. For many their claimed expertise may be based more on the need for finding significance in power than on actual knowledge or experience.

We are socialized to trust experts early in our lives; schools are a primary inculcator of expertism in our society. American schools teach children to be obedient to those in charge. They also discourage questioning the way things are done. Reward, and therefore worth, comes to those who do exactly as they are told without questioning or challenging. Rarely are students allowed to have input into administrative and curriculum decisions that concretely affect their lives. They are expected to conform to the idea that teachers and principals and deans always know what is best. The schools thus train us to follow directions instead of training us to question, challenge, and take responsibility for our decisions and our actions.

We are so socialized to trust the experts that we begin to trust everyone who appears to be an expert. Someone with a uniform, title, or important position seems to us worth trusting even if we know nothing about the person's credentials.

A study in 1974 found that people on the street obeyed a request by a person in a guard's uniform almost twice as often as the same request by a person in street clothes. "The uniform... significantly affected obedience, among old and young, men and women alike. In every situation, the pedestrians were more obedient to the high-authority figure, the guard.... Clearly, power was related to the type of uniform."[2] Police uniforms, lab coats, and business suits command authority because uniforms are among the influential symbols of expertism.

In almost all aspects of our lives we are told to trust the experts. The experts tell us that we must buy this or that in order to lead the good life, so we do. When there is an accident at a nuclear power plant, we are told that the experts say there is no threat to the public. Every year during budget hearings, experts tell us that the Soviets are beating us in the arms race; thus we must spend billions of dollars more on military buildup. We allocate the funds even though we do not understand the situation or know whether or not the claim is true.

When we hand over the major decisions to the experts, we weaken the democratic process. We become more and more a "technocracy," a government run by technologists or experts. In a technocracy we are taught to think we are acting responsibly when we just do what is expected of us. "Responsibility" becomes merely doing one's "duty" or acting in conformity to the norm. On the other hand, government by the people means that we have to make the decisions. As an electorate we have to be concerned enough and informed enough to be able to participate in deciding matters responsibly. True responsibility must include gathering the facts, weighing the situation, making our own decision, and acting on it, trusting that we have chosen the most humane course.

In American society we are often too busy or too self-focused to take the time and energy required for true responsibility. By handing the problems over to those who are only too glad to unburden us, we relinquish our democratic power. We let someone else make the decisions so that we can be free to get on with "our own thing."

Thus, we separate ourselves from the power of government and entrust the decisions to experts.

We founded this nation on an ideal of rule by the people, a desire to avoid centralized government, and a love of the liberty of democracy. However, we have increasingly come to have rule by "experts." As a result we have a highly centralized government that has much more unquestioned power than King George III ever dreamed of.

Consumer Ethic

Americans waste *more energy than most of the world* uses. —Bruce Birch and Larry Rasmussen

The search for extrinsic worth is also expressed in what can be called the "consumer ethic." This ethic dictates that "more is always better" and that the way to have "more" is through consuming. The original meaning of consume is "to devour or destroy completely." Though we don't usually make the connection, the appropriateness of the label for the buyers in a growth economy is clear. Since more is always better, regardless of how much we have already, we consume endlessly—buying and spending, accumulating and wasting with no apparent end in sight. In the words of psychoanalyst Erich Fromm, "The consumer is the eternal suckling crying for the bottle."[3]

Since we perceive that worth can be implied from our material wealth, the more we own the more importance we feel we have. We compete to have the most and the best because this increases the significance we think we gain. We conform to the societal standards of what, when, and how much we should buy according to consumer experts. The amount of worth we have is felt to be relative to how we compare with the expectations.

The consumer ethic elicits an unequal distribution of wealth. We tend to think of "standard of living" as referring to "the ability to buy whatever we want." By this definition, the American standard of living is quite high. But this constant search for worth from the department store and showroom wastes the energy and money that could be used to raise our standard of living in other, more humane ways. As a result, the U.S. does not rank very well compared to other industrial nations in terms of literacy, infant mortality, crime rate, and the percentage of citizens who are unemployed, poor, and homeless.

More and more for us means less and less for others. Though this may bother our sense of justice, we are protected from the implications of this by dualistic thinking and the exclusionist attitude. These factors enable us to tell ourselves that some are more deserving than others and that we deserve what we have. We also have the idea that the less others have the better we look in comparison and the more worth we have as a result. Thus we have a society in which the top one half of 1 percent own 35 percent of the wealth. We have a world in which the U.S., comprised of just 6 percent of the world's population, uses approximately 30 percent of the world's resources consumed every year.

The consumer ethic enables massive waste and exploitation of resources. The worth we think we gain through such over-production and over-consumption is so vitally important to us that it evidently seems worth the destruction of the environment and the extinction of species. This is egocentrism in its worst expression. Not only are we willing to sacrifice the existence of other living things on the altar of our personal significance, but we also seem just as disdainful and apathetic about our own future. Egocentrism is focused on the self, here and now. Long-range perception and planning is difficult with such distorted vision. We either don't care or we try to ignore the fact that on a planet of limited resources the spiral toward obtaining more and more means that eventually there will be few resources left.

Instrumentalism

> *We are so obsessed with* doing *that we have no time and no imagination left for* being.... *As a result, men are valued not for what they are but for what they* do *or what they* have — *for their usefulness.*
>
> —Thomas Merton

The consumer ethic is supplemented and reinforced by an attitude of instrumentalism. Instrumentalism dictates that people or things are of worth only if, and only to the extent that, they are useful to me. This attitude is not often stated or acknowledged openly, especially in reference to other people, but we act on it more than we would like to admit. Clearly an expression of egocentrism, instrumentalism causes us to relate to everything around us in terms of our own needs, desires, goals. To this way of thinking, a tree is uncut lumber, a work of art is a saleable product, and a person is a role.

Instrumentalism in terms of the environment means that unless we use natural resources (land, animals, minerals, vegetation), they go to waste. The only worth the natural world has is the function it can fill for us. This attitude paves the way for gross exploitation, extinction of species, and destruction of the environment.

Instrumentalism extends to the people around us as well. It can be seen in the independent/dependent character of egocentric relationships in which the relationship is seen as a way of gaining or protecting our worth. Econo-egocentrism reduces the people we have contact with to "roles"; that they, too, are selves is eclipsed in the importance of the function they fill for us. It is easy in our society for another to become only the person who checks us out at the supermarket, the telephone repair person, the teacher, the student, the "street person," the boss, the workers. We are socialized to relate to each other as mechanical roles that function to sell to us, buy from us, render a service for us, irritate and inconvenience us, work for us, pay us.

> From an instrumental perspective, a person is valued because he or she is a good worker, or provider, or sex object, or is useful in meeting one's needs in some other fashion. Everyone knows someone about whom you can say, "Oh, he's only interested in you if you can do something for him, otherwise you don't exist." This is an instrumental outlook. People and objects are sacred in the sociological sense when, apart from what instrumental use they serve, they are valued for themselves.[4]

Instrumentalism is directly related to the abstraction of work that has occurred in industrialized, consumer-oriented society. As workers we are often uninvolved in the final product or result of our labors; we are "simply performing a function in return for money.... In the process, we have become alienated from our work and from one another as we compete for the opportunities to make money."[5]

Increasingly, we find ourselves involved in "invented work,"

work that we neither enjoy nor feel produces something that is important to survival or the enhancement of life. We may suspect but dread to admit that our time and energy is used up in endeavors that have come into being simply to pamper our egocentrism or someone else's bank account. It is almost too frightening to consider that the way we spend forty-plus hours a week might have little real significance. But often it seems all too true at seven o'clock Monday morning.

Invented work involves viewing the worker through the perspective of instrumentalism. The reduction of creativity to role and function also diminishes something "human" in the worker. "To deny someone necessary and fulfilling work is to deny that person's being created in the image of God."[6] We should be able to use our energy, time, and creativity doing what we enjoy, creating something we feel is useful or beautiful, or easing suffering for ourselves and others. Instead, econo-egocentrism pushes us to get involved in invented work, doing something we don't enjoy or producing something we don't believe in. We do this out of a desire to "be somebody" as our society defines it and because those are the sorts of jobs available to us. Thus, instrumentalism has helped to create an alienated, apathetic populace, unhealthy relationships, and a separation from our environment that is leading to its, and thus our own, ultimate destruction.

Most of us don't feel that it is right or reasonable to destroy the environment, just as most of us don't feel it is right to use violence or coercion, conform to someone else's opinion, or treat others as inferiors. We don't feel that it is right to use more than our share of resources, to spend millions of dollars constructing machines of death while children are malnourished, or to compete tooth-and-nail in order to "make it" economically and socially.

We don't mean for our behavior to be destructive, but sometimes we find we can't avoid it. We feel trapped in a social order where it seems the only way to function effectively is to act in ways we fear are immoral, ungenerous, or unkind.

At times such actions seem totally beyond our control. We walk past homeless people on the street every day without offering to help because there are so many that we feel totally overwhelmed and numbed by the enormity of the problem. We buy from or invest in companies that despoil the environment or that have involvements in countries with inhumane, unjust governments. We don't wish to add to air pollution but most of us find it almost impossible to avoid driving many places every day.

There are few, if any, people in the world who, like Saturday morning cartoon villains, set out to "do evil." But we find we end up doing, or being involved in, unjust, insensitive, and unkind acts all the same. We are caught in this situation because we feel such a deep-seated need to prove our significance. With our perception distorted by egocentrism, this need appears to be all-important. Other issues and considerations seem so small and insignificant in comparison to finding significance, to earning and protecting our worth.

This distorted perception is not our fault. We are socialized to think this way and almost everything around us reinforces this attitude. Our econo-egocentric worldview pervades our society, convincing us that in order to really have a meaningful life we must find worth at any cost. Even when we sense that this is not the most functional or compassionate way to exist, we feel we can't help but go along. No matter how much we regret it, there just doesn't seem to be any choice. That's the way the world works; we have to earn our worth.

See below chapter 14, "Trying It on for Size," pages 133ff., nos. 6, 9, and 10.

See below chapter 15, "Food for Thought," pages 168ff., nos. 1, 3, and 67.

CHAPTER 6

Intrinsically Ours

Value has already been given to everything in creation by God's birthing it into being.
—Elizabeth Dodson Gray

The extrinsic worth way of thinking is so pervasive and entrenched that it is difficult to consider an alternative. With the idea of extrinsic worth serving as the bedrock that underlies and shapes the geography of our society, how could any alternative be possible? It seems as indisputable and absolute as the actual geologic bedrock. But underneath that bedrock there is constant motion and change that occasionally breaks through and bubbles forth. The bedrock is merely a thin layer that we like to think is solid and immutable.

Occasionally acts of compassion, cooperation, and appreciation of life, acts not motivated by the quest for extrinsic worth, break through and bubble forth. Could this be a clue that extrinsic worth is not as absolute as it seems? Is there another way?

Such acts are evidence of the continued influence of the first tradition. These alternative values persist as a subordinate countertheme to econo-egocentrism, suggesting that a different perception and understanding are possible. As a system of values and understandings, the first tradition has the potential to develop into a worldview in its own right. It also offers an alternative view of human worth. The values of interdependence, cooperation, and responsibility do not arise from an understanding of human worth as extrinsic. Instead they are rooted in the idea that humans are of worth *intrinsically.*

This perspective holds that we do not need to provide our own significance. Our significance is built in. We are of value because we exist and only for that reason. We are important because we came into existence and because we are an integral part of the entire universe. We are of worth from the moment we come into being. Our worth is inherently ours; nothing can take it away.

We are socialized to think in terms of having things, knowledge, or skills in order to establish our significance or of accomplishing certain deeds in order to have a meaningful life. Because of this, it seldom occurs to us that we might be of worth just because we exist or that life is meaningful in and of itself. This perspective, however, is a viable understanding of human worth.

There are many alternatives to the philosophy of extrinsic worth. One is that of intrinsic worth: humans are born with worth that can neither be lost nor increased. A second alternative is to believe that humans have no worth and can never hope to gain any. Another is to believe that humans are born with worth but can lose it later. Or we could believe that some humans are born with more worth than other humans. Intrinsic worth is not the only alternative to the idea of extrinsic worth, but it is one that we are already familiar with through the influence of the first tradition. It is also a very positive and creative alternative that offers the possibility of healing and reshaping our troubled society.

Instead of the "having" formula, which lays out certain conditions for us to follow in order to have significance, the intrinsic worth idea has no conditions other than "Be!" There is no formula for being, only encouragement to accept who we are as unique selves who are important because we *are.* There is no push for us to "become somebody"; we are somebody already. And not because of what we own, or know, or can do, but because we exist in this universe.

In the extrinsic worth view of things, we can work hard and increase our importance. But we can also lose our importance. In the intrinsic worth view of life, we cannot add anything to our importance, because we are already as important as it is possible for a human being to be. Neither can we lose our importance, for it is built in. We cannot lose our identity because it comes with our existence. We cannot lose the meaning of life because the meaning of life is life itself.

People who understand their worth as intrinsic do not feel pressured to undergo change in order to impress others, or even themselves. Change results from being able to appreciate their own potential for growth, mentally, physically, and spiritually. Such persons are enabled to affirm the possibilities to be found in life's limitations and, at the same time, concede the limitations in the midst of life's possibilities. They are able to celebrate their own lives, the lives of others, and all of Creation.

The extrinsic worth view says: as long as I own, or I know, or I do, I am somebody. From the intrinsic worth viewpoint we don't need these qualifiers. The intrinsic worth idea, echoing the universe, says only, "I am!"

Intrinsic Worth and Democracy

We hold these truths to be self-evident...
—Declaration of Independence

To those of us steeped in the convictions of extrinsic worth the concept of intrinsic worth may seem bizarre or ludicrous. It may appear idealistic and a sure route to self-destruction for anyone surrounded by an econo-egocentric culture. And it may seem highly impractical to those of us convinced that the only way to have worth is the old-fashioned way: you earn it!

However, the idea of intrinsic worth is by no means a new concept. It can be found as a thread in the tapestry of religions and philosophies through the ages. As with the first tradition of American values, the thread of intrinsic worth has seldom, if ever, been dominant in a society. The idea of intrinsic worth undermines hierarchical power. Therefore it is a wonder that it has not been totally driven out of our collective understanding by the extrinsic worth philosophy, which has generally had the spears and the guns and the police power at its service. Yet it has surfaced again and again in different forms and expressions, in Celtic and Saxon traditions, in twelfth-century civic efforts, and in medieval Swiss villages. From many sources it has continued to influence our thoughts and feelings and therefore our society.

With the experiments in democracy in the eighteenth century, the worth of each individual began to be taken seriously in practical politics. The basis for human rights is intrinsic worth: to say that each person has basic inalienable rights is to say that each person deserves those rights, that each person is of worth. Democracy must be based on the presumption of intrinsic worth. Government by the people is nonsensical if it is believed that only those with money or influence are of enough worth to warrant their having political power.

These early democratic experiments were obviously flawed because women, slaves, and others were not included in the political process. But the basic perspective of inalienable rights and equality was nevertheless revolutionary in its expression of intrinsic worth in an extrinsic worth society.

Unconditional Love

You have Cosmic permission to be who you are!
—Joseph Mathews

The idea of intrinsic worth is also a vital factor in the traditions of both Jews and Christians. The message that we are of worth, that we are loved, that we are important because we are part of God's glorious Creation, is found throughout the scriptures.

Biblical reference to the idea of intrinsic worth is found most often in the phrase "God's steadfast love." The love God feels for humankind doesn't have to be earned. God may not approve of all our actions and may leave us to reap what we sow (Prov. 1:31, Jer. 6:19), but when it comes to God's *love* there are no "if's" or conditions. God's love is everlasting.

There are a number of Psalms (89, 100, 103, 107, 130, 136, in particular) that declare that God's steadfast love will endure forever. In Isaiah 54:10 God declares that though the mountains and hills be worn down, God's steadfast love will not depart. In verse 8 God says, "... with everlasting love I will have compassion on you." "Everlasting" means that God's love will never be taken away. No matter what. "His steadfast love endures forever" (Ps. 136). Nothing can change the situation. God's love for human beings is unconditional.

This idea may be difficult to comprehend or may even be offensive for those who think in terms of extrinsic worth, because it means they do not have to do anything to earn God's love. Those of us who are used to gaining, earning, winning our way through life are faced with the realization that the biggest ego-enhancement ever, God's love, has been ours all along. It doesn't have to be worked for. It can't be lost. And, most frustrating of all, *it is shared equally.* God's love for us comes like the rain, to the just and the unjust alike. It is given, with no strings attached, to those who have earned social "respectability" and status, and to those who have not.

Human beings are referred to as being created in the image of God (Gen. 1:27). We are created a "little less than God" and crowned "with glory and honor" (Ps. 8:5). "Royal dignity was yours from the day you were born, on the holy mountains, royal from the womb, from the dawn of your earliest days" (Ps. 110:3 NJB). Clearly, these writings do not condemn us for our lack of worth, nor exhort us to struggle to gain importance. Instead they joyously announce that our "royalty" is a birthright, that dignity and worth are ours inherently.

The message of intrinsic worth is just as strong in the New Testament. Paul, in his letter to the church at Rome, affirms the idea of God's unconditional love when he says that nothing will separate us from the love of God (8:39). This love is a gift that cannot be worked for (Eph. 2:8–9). If we still entertain any ideas of trying to be good enough to earn God's love, he undercuts that by saying that God loves us even while we are sinners (Rom. 5:8).

"Grace" is the word used to point to an event in an individual's life when God's unconditional love is truly realized. If we have such an experience we are never quite the same. It is an experience of alternation; the world seems different with "new dimensions and colors" and life is never the same again. No matter what happens we can never ignore the awareness that God loves us with "no strings attached." We really know that the struggle to find a sense of significance is over.

Jesus himself lived out of an intrinsic worth understanding. He did not spend his life trying to obtain those things that society said would give him worth. Neither did he seem to differentiate between the "successful" in society and those who had fallen through the cracks. He befriended tax collectors and prostitutes and others who were considered the most unworthy in society. He regarded all persons as equally loved by God. This confused and angered those who felt that, through their successes, they were worth more, that they had earned significance in the eyes of God. Even the disciples disputed who was to be the "greatest." But Jesus refused such designations: "Whoever humbles himself like this child, he is the greatest in the kingdom of heaven" (Matt. 18:4).

A Split in Theology

> *Christianity reared people full of sanguine instinct, ...cruel and barbarous in the juridical understanding of Christianity, a severe method creating a genuine spiritual terror. But one may contrast to the juridical understanding a deeper understanding of Christianity as the revelation of love and freedom. The human being is called to be creator and participator in the work of God's creation. It is God's call addressed to human beings toward which they must respond freely. God does not need submissive and obedient slaves, always trembling and egoistically preoccupied with themselves. God needs sons and daughters, free and creative, loving and daring. Humanity frightfully distorted the image of God and ascribed to him its own distorted and sinful psychology.*
>
> —Nicholas Berdyaev

Jesus' message was taken into societies that had worldviews that were strongly dualistic. Instead of understanding Creation as good, these worldviews saw Creation divided into good and evil, right and wrong, positive and negative. Light was associated with good, dark with evil. Things spiritual were good and things physical were bad. One had to focus one's thoughts and actions on things of the spirit and avoid things of the body in order to have any hope of improvement of the condition of the soul. Since everyone had a body, which made demands from time to time for food and sleep and sex, it was easy to conclude that everyone was naturally inclined toward bad things. This made the struggle for salvation seem very difficult for most.

This, of course, was the same old bad news people had been telling each other for centuries. As a result, there developed two messages within Christianity. There were many going around sharing the bad news that you had to prove yourself to God, or else. And there were not so many going around sharing the good news that God loves us unconditionally. Thus, all along, we have had two conflicting theologies: the dominant one of extrinsic worth and the often unrealized one of intrinsic worth.

The extrinsic theology has been the prevailing view of the human condition in western Christendom for 1900 years. Through these centuries people learned that they were not intrinsically worthy, not guaranteed God's everlasting love, and not bound for

Heaven unless they could behave in such a way that would win God's love for themselves.

This subversion of the message of Jesus is not surprising because all the cultures into which the early missionaries went were based on the perspective of extrinsic worth. In the West, the patriarchal cultures of the Romans, Goths, Vandals, Franks, Vikings, and other peoples were built on competition and violence and trying to prove themselves worthy enough to gain something from their gods. Although these peoples eventually became a part of institutional Christianity, they brought much of their traditional cultures with them. This kept them from being able to understand fully the idea of God's unconditional love.

Here and there, however, there were those who, in spite of the prevailing worldview, understood Creation as good and human beings as a part of that good Creation. One culture that made it possible for people to understand this good news was that of the Celts. They had a strong tradition of tribal warfare, cattle raids, and besting one another in everything from fighting to singing. But they also had a sense of the mystic which, combined with a deep love of nature, allowed them to appreciate the concepts of intrinsic worth and the blessing of Creation.

From the Celtic lands came influential thinkers and leaders: Patrick, Columba, John Scotus Erigena, and even Pelagius, who was excommunicated because the Roman mind could not understand and appreciate the Celtic worldview. For some four hundred years, Celtic missionaries, chiefly from Ireland, streamed onto the continent. These evangelists, known as *peregrini,* counseled kings, established churches, and influenced the thinking of layfolk as well as the monastics. It is thought by some that their understanding of Creation and appreciation of nature greatly influenced Francis of Assisi and the Rhineland Mystics.

One of these mystics was the notable abbess Hildegard, who lived in the eleventh century. She was not only a theologian but also a physician, naturalist, poet, musician, and debater with kings and popes. Later there was Mechtild, who was of the Beguines. This was an association of lay women who sought to be on their own in service to the poor without being dominated by men either within the church or without. There was Meister Eckhart, a fourteenth-century Dominican who believed that every person is an aristocrat, that every person is noble, "born from the infinite depths of the divine nature and the divine wilderness."[1] His ideas of democracy were quite threatening to the nobles and those clerics in the higher echelons of the church. Influenced by this theology of blessing was Lady Julian in fourteenth-century England, whose writings express a joyous reverence for all of Creation.

This theology had its influence on the Reformation, as Luther and others saw the implications of God's unconditional love. The Reformation influenced some of the Enlightenment thinkers in their consideration of the concept that all humans are equal before "Nature and Nature's God." In this way, the intrinsic worth idea, however incompletely understood, came to be a part of the communocentric tradition in the United States.

Creation as Blessing

> *I know well that heaven and earth and all creation are great, generous and beautiful and good.... God's goodness fills all his creatures and all his blessed world full, and endlessly overflows in them.... God is everything which is good, as I see it, and the goodness which everything has is God.* —Julian of Norwich

The idea that humans are of worth just because they exist goes hand-in-hand with the understanding that Creation is a blessing. We are of worth because Creation is of worth and we are part of Creation. It's that simple. The Creation story in Genesis is not a sad tale of the beginning of meaningless existence. It is a joyful account of God creating something wonderful. "And God saw everything that he had made, and behold, it was very good" (Gen. 1:31).

Creating the universe was pleasing to God—and still is. God's creative energy, the divine Word, was not a one-time event but is an ongoing, dynamic process that we, and all things around us, are a part of. "The *Word* is living, being, spirit, all verdant greening, all creativity.... This *Word* manifests itself in every creature."[2] The Creator not only saw that it *was* good, but continues to see that it *is* good! Life itself is worthwhile and exciting; life needs no meaning beyond itself.

According to Klaus Westermann, the Hebrews celebrated the "mighty acts" of God that had delivered them, but it was their understanding of God's blessing through Creation that they experienced day by day, year by year. They received life and with it children and rain and food and pleasure, all gifts of God through Creation.[3]

The understanding that Creation is a blessing removes the fear created by the dualism of Good versus Evil. So many ancient myths, children's stories, and recent horror films reinforce the idea that part of the universe is bad and part is good and that we are caught in the eternal struggle between the two. But if we believe the story in Genesis that Creation is good, and what the celebratory mystics tell us about the blessedness of the universe, we will see that there is no such dualism, no such eternal struggle. *The universe is good, and it has no opposite.*

The blessedness of Creation and the worth of our own existence are given us as a gift to be received in joy, savored, and appreciated. But, unfortunately, our response is often to reject, denounce, or deny this great gift. This we do simply by believing that the only significance worth having is extrinsic. If we believe that our worth comes through our own actions instead of through being a part of Creation, then we focus on ourselves, devalue the rest of Creation, and miss the true meaningfulness of life. Feeling that we are not blessed suggests that we may doubt the blessedness of Creation as well.

Sin, Salvation, and Intrinsic Worth

> *Since the sin of separateness is not an act of disobedience, it does not need to be* forgiven. *But it does need to be* healed; *and love, not acceptance of punishment, is the healing factor.* —Erich Fromm

Rejecting our inherent worth separates us from Creation. This separation is what we call "sin." Paul Tillich describes sin as separation from God, from others, from ourselves.[4] In other words, sin is failing to understand ourselves as a part of Creation; it is being unable to appreciate Creation as a gift and as a blessing. The Greek word for sin is "*hamartia,*" which means "missing the mark," i.e., missing the understanding of the meaning of life, focusing on the wrong things, and thereby missing what is really important.

When we separate ourselves from Creation, and thus from entering into the blessing that is Creation, we separate ourselves from realizing the meaningfulness of life itself, from experiencing the worth that our existence has. We condemn ourselves to a life of searching—for meaning, for significance, for worth, for "salvation," for a vague something we're not quite sure of but know we lack.

This insufficiency may cause us to feel meaningless and nihilistic, believing that life contains nothing more than an unending search for significance. If we feel our insufficiency is our own fault, it can instill feelings of guilt. We feel we must have failed to do or be something we should. No matter how hard we strive for perfection, we remain imperfect. Creation may be a blessing but we feel we have failed to live up to some standard. We think we are imperfect and sinful and thus we do not deserve to celebrate the blessing of Creation. We feel we must prove that we are worthy of such a gift. Surrounded by the gift and blessing of Creation, we deny ourselves the joy of accepting it. We cut ourselves off from that which is really meaningful and waste our lives trying to find worth and meaning in our own constructions.

Creation is a blessing and our lives are intrinsically worthy. Nothing can change that; we cannot lose our worth. But we *can* miss out on the meaningfulness of life if we don't allow ourselves to see it. We *can* lose the chance to experience being a significant part of a blessed Creation if we never open ourselves to it nor even admit the possibility.

Our worth is ours intrinsically and the blessing that is life is right before us. We have been given these wonderful gifts and gifts have no strings attached. But it is up to us to realize they are there, accept them, and allow them to become part of our lives. Jesus announces that "the Reign of Heaven is among you." It is not something we have to earn. It's here; we only have to realize it. Creation is spread out before us like a great banquet. If we were not worthy would it be offered in this way?

This is our salvation—to realize the blessing that is life, to be saved from our self-imposed denial of Creation. Salvation is not something we earn, something to have. It is realizing our worth and life's blessing were there and possible all along. Salvation means overcoming the separation from Creation by realizing and accepting the worth and the blessing. Salvation means "at-one-ment," becoming one with Creation. Through this at-one-ment we realize that our lives are filled with wonder and excitement and beauty beyond all imagining. We understand that "salvation is enchanted existence."[5] Once we discover this wonder we can glory in existence, instead of just existing for future glory.

The Necessity of Celebration

To praise God one must live... and to live, one must enjoy life; one must enjoy life in spite of life.
—Elie Wiesel

We have been given a great gift, invited to partake of a wondrous banquet. It is for us to be good guests and appreciate the fare, rejoice in the experience, and enjoy ourselves thoroughly. It is what any generous host would request.

We are called to celebrate—celebrate Creation, celebrate our existence, celebrate just to celebrate. Too often the church, and other societal forces, have told us that enjoying ourselves is sinful. We have been programmed to think that if it "feels good" it must be wrong. These condemning "voices" cause us to restrain our joy, our celebration, our pleasure. They justify their condemnation with their idea of extrinsic worth, which tells us that we must be "good," and not necessarily happy, in order to have worth. What we need is to relearn celebration: savoring life and letting ourselves enjoy what is given.

This does not imply that "if it feels good" we can "do it" to the detriment of our health or the infringement of the dignity of others. Seeing each part of Creation as unique and significant will keep us from falling into the trap of feeling that since we are loved by God we can do anything we want. Our valuing of all parts of Creation will not allow us to manipulate other persons and other species to our own purposes.

The Bible is full of images of celebration: banquets of fine wine and bounteous food, joyful music, praises sung to the Creator. Though usually portrayed as a somber, reserved sort, Jesus must have known the goodness of celebration. He insured that at least one party he attended could continue even after the wine ran out.

In the act of celebrating we rejoice in and enter into the blessed wonder of Creation. "In celebration we forget the superficial in order to remember the deep."[6] Celebration is transcendence and it is at-one-ment. Through celebrating we move beyond ourselves to join in the celebration of Creation.

Celebration is not only our goal, the end to which we strive, but it is also the means for reaching that end. It is fruitless to believe that we cannot celebrate until all the problems in the world are solved. We cannot be people of God if we are not a celebrating people. "This is the day which the Lord has made; let us rejoice and be glad in it" (Ps. 118:24). "Behold, now is the acceptable time; behold, now is the day of salvation" (2 Cor. 6:2). We cannot be truly aware of the blessing of Creation without rejoicing in it. We cannot bring about the re-creation of the world without bringing it recreation.

It may seem that the problems facing the world are so serious that it is silly and even dangerous to celebrate. To celebrate would be to fiddle while Rome burns or to stick our heads in the sand. But celebration is not an escape; it is a vital part of solving problems, of realizing the Reign of Heaven in our midst.

We work and hope and pray that all might have lives they can appreciate and enjoy. How does it help if we don't appreciate and enjoy our own? If we ourselves do not feel at-one-ment with Creation, how can we help anyone else feel it? Letting our lives slip away uncelebrated, unaffirmed, unrejoiced is denying the blessing of Creation. We must say "yes" to our intrinsic worth before its power can fill our lives.

We cannot wait for all our problems to be solved before we appreciate what's been given us. We also *need* celebration in order to solve these problems. Working to relieve suffering without celebrating life just brings on feelings of depression and frustration. We can't relieve suffering from a distance; we must share in it. And we can't truly share in the pain and suffering without also sharing in the joy. We bond ourselves deeply to the experiences of others to become a truly human family. This oneness of feeling is found and expressed most deeply and profoundly in shared celebration.

Intrinsic Worth in Our Lives

God can never be insulted by us except we act against our own well-being. —Thomas Aquinas

If we realize that life is meaningful in and of itself we need no longer search for meaning through material wealth or personal success. We find that the glory and blessing of Creation are meaning enough. "Nothing that is necessary for life is lacking."[7] What we value, our goals, our very attitude toward life thus changes. We realize along with Abraham Heschel that "just to be is a blessing. Just to live is holy."[8]

Trusting that our worth is intrinsic can dramatically change how we think about ourselves, others, and life in general. If we trust that our significance is part of our being, we can feel that we are special, that we are important just as we are. If we don't need to prove our worth to others we can be comfortable with who we are and not try to disguise ourselves or become "someone else" by conforming. When we no longer feel that our worth depends on whether we are "right" or "wrong" we can be free to express our true feelings and perspectives. When we no longer feel we must conform to a certain predetermined way of being we are liberated to discover our uniqueness.

If we grant that our worth cannot be added to, we can appreciate ourselves without feeling we are bucking for more worth. We will be able to celebrate our attributes — our talents, our strengths, our sensitivity — without feeling we are being conceited.

If we grant that our worth cannot be diminished, we can deal honestly with what we feel are our shortcomings. We don't have to fear being less worthy. We can let go of the quest for perfection. We can stop trying to live up to someone else's expectations. We can see our strengths and weaknesses as parts of our wholeness. Feelings of guilt and inadequacy will no longer have the same power over us.

We don't have to be pressured into using our creativity in trying to be important, seeking significance, or competing for worth in any way possible. Instead we can spend our time, energy, and resources creatively, compassionately, joyfully. We can use our creativity for enjoyment and expression instead of having to use it to compete or create a "product."

When we no longer fear losing our worth because of "being different" (i.e., unique), we can be free to risk new ideas and new activities. No longer feeling inhibited, we can give full reign to our creativity. No longer constrained by dualistic thinking and the fear of losing our worth, we can celebrate the ambiguities and paradoxes of life.

If we trust that worth is intrinsic then we can see those around us as having intrinsic worth as well. We can treat them with respect, as equals. Realizing our inherent equality, we will no longer either look down on or idolize other people. We may disapprove or applaud their actions, but their actions in no way change their equal worthiness as human beings.

Because our worth is not dependent on comparison with others, we will have no need of "digging holes" for them to fall into. Knowing we are all intrinsically worthy, we find there is no need to compete or compare. We can cooperate and help others without feeling we are risking our worth. We can celebrate their accomplishments instead of feeling jealous.

We will have no need to fear falling in holes others have dug for us. Knowing their own worth is intrinsic and secure, other people will feel no need to dig holes. Even if there are those still operating out of the idea of extrinsic worth, their hole-digging will have no effect upon us. We "fall in a hole" only when we feel we have lost some worth. Trusting in our intrinsic, inalienable worth, we no longer need to worry about this "threat."

Since others will feel no need to compete with us we can trust them and not suspect their intentions. We need not fear being vulnerable because other people, knowing their own worth cannot be lost, should feel no need to take advantage of us. Trusting those around us can enable us to be more open and honest. We can work cooperatively with patience and trust because no one is out to get ahead of another. We can feel free to be caring and compassionate, rejoicing in the "be-ing" of others instead of comparing and competing with their "have-ing."

With the realization of our intrinsic worth will also come a new perspective on all of life. Each part of the universe is unique, and we are not exceptions. Each of us is like no other person or thing in the universe. Each of us has no more, and no less, value than any other person or thing. If we agree with physicist Brian Swimme that the universe has labored for 15 billion years to produce you and me, we must grant that it has also worked 20 billion years to produce the dandelion on our lawn, the snow on the pines, the spider, and the horseshoe crab. The same number of years has gone into producing all that we like and all that we don't like, and everything in the universe has been presented to us as a unique gift to be cherished. Since the entire universe is part of the goodness of Creation, everything in it, each subatomic particle, is of ultimate significance, and so are we. Creation is a blessing, life is meaningful in and of itself, and we are of worth intrinsically and unconditionally.

See below chapter 14, "Trying It on for Size," pages 133ff., nos. 24, 32, and 78.

See below chapter 15, "Food for Thought," pages 168ff., nos. 2, 19, 30, and 69.

CHAPTER 7

An Alternative Worldview . . .

"Seeing" things differently means seeing things not seen before, comprehending things not comprehended before, judging things differently from before. Some things that once did not make sense inside the old perspective now do. And some things that did *make sense inside the old perspective are now the occasion for smiling and shaking one's head. The once "inconceivable" now appears possible, in imagination at least, and often in fact. A new perspective is frequently the key to new ways of doing things.*

—Bruce Birch and Larry Rasmussen

If the ethic of intrinsic worth were to become commonly accepted in American society, it would totally and radically change our perspective on, and understanding of, our lives and the world we live in. We would thus have a new worldview, one based on a shared understanding and acceptance of the intrinsic, unconditional nature of human worth. This worldview would not be totally new to us; it would include many of the attitudes and behaviors of the first tradition of American values. The potential for such a worldview is illustrated by the persistence and survival of the first tradition, despite the overpowering influence of econo-egocentrism. We will refer to this worldview as "geo-communocentrism"—"communocentrism" because the focus would be on community, and "geo" because it would be inclusive of the global community of humans and all living things.

Geo-communocentrism, like econo-egocentrism, is not a *thing.* It is people treating people in certain ways. These ways of relating are very different from those included in econo-egocentrism, but people are quite capable of acting and thinking in many different ways. The behaviors and attitudes described in chapter 6 could arise as a matter of course in a society with a geo-communocentric worldview. From an econo-egocentric perspective, however, these possibilities and projections may seem idealistic or utopian: "Yes, it would be nice if we all acted that way, but nobody will do it. People just aren't like that!" It is crucial to remember that we are talking about a very radical change. We are not enjoining everyone to be good, to act morally. If social problems had such a simple solution things would have changed centuries ago. What we are talking about is a change in the very way we perceive reality, in the way we understand our identity and the meaning in our lives.

Such fundamental changes will naturally have far-reaching effects. Some of these effects may seem unrealistic; this is because they are beyond our present understanding of "reality." They *are* unrealistic in an econo-egocentric worldview, where human worth is understood to be extrinsic. But if this is not our understanding, everything is perceived differently. *If we are working out of a different frame of reference, our idea of what is unrealistic and what is realistic will change!*

History and personal experience can show that one significant change will open up the potential for many others. The single invention of the steam engine suddenly made previous impossibilities possible. It changed our idea of what was real and what was just fanciful dreaming. The publication of the Declaration of Independence excited people in other nations, giving them a vision of great possibilities. Changing our worldview would have an even more profound effect.

In order to imagine what might be possible within a new worldview we must remove ourselves from the framework of the old one. If we look at the possible results of an intrinsic worth worldview from the stance of extrinsic worth they are certain to seem senseless and irrational. If we are convinced of the vital need to earn worth at any cost, the idea of being of worth intrinsically and therefore needing to do nothing to gain or protect our significance seems foolish and utopian. We must look at the possibilities and potential results of intrinsic worth from the perspective of intrinsic worth in order to see how realistic and promising they really are.

These possibilities and potential results may not have existed or been experienced before. We know of no examples of worldviews based on intrinsic worth. The idea has had a degree of influence in scattered instances, such as the American first tradition. But it has rarely, if ever, been fully expressed or manifest in a social order. Thus, if we are to come to some idea of what a geo-communocentric society would be like, we must creatively and constructively imagine it.

Envisioning

"Would you tell me please, which way I ought to go from here?" "That depends a good deal on where you want to get to," said the Cat. —Lewis Carroll

Imagination is often discounted in our society. It is considered appropriate for children, artists, inventors, and economists, but for the rest of us it is deemed impractical or even harmful, certainly a waste of time. We seldom realize that imagination can be a dynamic, creative force in our lives. We are a species of artists, dreamers, storytellers, creators. It is not only our fiction writers who create through imagination. Every one of us does so when we daydream, come up with a solution to a problem, or plan for the future. We open new doors and new possibilities when we decide to get married, raise a family, pursue a dream, or go to Antarctica to study penguins. The plans don't always turn out as we expected, but just by envisioning them we make them possibilities, real possibilities. Because it is not tied down by convention, imagination can discover and even create possibilities that never existed before.

Rational thought and imagination are complementary and work best when used together. Reason offers form and function; imagination provides life and power. Using them together avoids both the stagnation of pure rationality and the ethereal nature of unchannelled imagination. This combination can give rise to creativity that is "realistic," that is relevant to, and functional in, this world.

It is this combination we use when we constructively imagine alternatives to our worldview and social framework. We must ask ourselves what might be the logical outcome of such changes. What can we creatively imagine as possible? In this way we begin to envision what a society based on intrinsic worth could be like.

The "envisioning" process serves several functions. First, we realize that the seemingly small change from extrinsic to intrinsic worth could actually lead to major, wide-scale adaptations and developments in our society. Second, seeing what might be possible motivates us to attempt the change. Having some idea of possible results offers much more incentive to break out of our old worldview than if we had no idea of what might occur. Third, through describing and outlining what we would like our society to be, envisioning provides some idea of which way we should go. If we don't know where we want to end up, or even what our possible choices are, it's hard to know how to get started. Envisioning goals and imagining potential results shows us what is possible, gives us an incentive to attempt the change, and provides a kind of map, or at least a general direction, to guide us into "new territory."

Envisioning what geo-communocentrism might be like is not just a mental exercise. The reason for changing our worldview is not because we're tired of it (though some of us probably are). The real need for change comes from the multitude of social, political, economic, and ecological problems that arise from econo-egocentrism.

Developing a new worldview would not solve all our problems. Unfortunately, there would be ecological devastation left as a legacy of our present way of thinking. We would have to figure out how to have efficient and functional democracy in a nation of over 245 million people. We would also be challenged to extend this democracy into the economy, developing economic structures that take each person's intrinsic worth into account.

In addition, geo-communocentrism would have many challenges of its own, such as developing social structures true to the new worldview. However, in all probability these difficulties would not threaten our survival as do the problems we now face with econo-egocentrism. The need to change is imperative; thus envisioning a new way is critical.

It is not the purpose of this book to provide a detailed description of what an intrinsic worth society would be like. We have an idea of the changes we think could occur and that we would like to see, but what seems possible to us may not be as clear to someone else. Likewise, we hope that each reader will envision things not included in this book. Human experiences, imagination, and knowledge run in different directions and thus can provide varying perspectives and insights. For this reason we must all envision for ourselves in order to develop a complete idea of our possibilities.

We also want to avoid setting ourselves up as "experts" by omnisciently dictating what changes would take place. Each of us has an equal ability to decide what we would like and to imagine what might be possible. Thus all of us can, and need to, put in our "two-cents worth" in an informal, democratic brainstorming process.

What we would like to do here is provide some idea of what *we* think would be possible if the American worldview were based on intrinsic rather than extrinsic worth. We hope to offer examples of what the envisioning process is like and to share our vision of the results it could produce. If it seems vague or incomplete, remember we are only in the envisioning process ourselves. Our experience is minute compared to the experience and knowledge of the entire society. It is a task for all of us to dream what is possible and work to make these possibilities real.

Interdependence

> *A citizen is a person who knows — and honors — the truth that he or she can fulfill himself or herself only as a member of a community.*
>
> —William A. Williams

Believing in our intrinsic worth shapes our attitude toward, and ways of relating to, others. If we understand that we do not have to struggle to find significance, we are more likely to interrelate with others without trying to use them, to whatever degree, for our advantage. If our need for worth is not the most important thing in our lives, we can more easily realize and understand the needs of others. We can thus focus on others as well as on ourselves. Free from our egocentrism, we can realize that we are all intricately interconnected. Geo-communocentrism is marked by the awareness of our interdependence.

Interdependence, as used here, is not a halfway point between dependence and independence. Nor does it refer to "mutual dependency," in the sense of two persons having to lean on each other. Interdependence means, rather, a "mutual reliance" and should carry with it the connotation of an active relationship based on mutual respect and shared responsibility for the common good. Interdependence means a "synergistic" endeavor, a confluencing of energy, envisioning, and creativity.

If we are not blinded by our egocentrism, we readily see that we are interconnected. We do not live as hermits in a vacuum; what I do affects you and what you do affects me. There is no avoiding this connection. We need to realize and accept the situation and begin to relate to each other as co-creators, companions in the struggles of life. Trusting in our intrinsic worth would offer us the freedom to be interdependent. If we do not have to struggle to compete for a sense of worth, then we can realize that giving and accepting support will in no way decrease or threaten our significance.

Admitting our mutual reliance, we would no longer strain relationships with clinging dependency or the façade of independence. Instead of associating with another person in an attempt to gain worth, we could enjoy intimacy and friendship as an end rather than a means to some kind of significance. Trusting that we are significant in the universe, we could feel free to be part of the community.

With geo-communocentrism as our worldview, an attitude of interdependence would have quite an effect on our society. Aware that anything we do affects others, we would have to take this into consideration in our plans and decisions.

The constant battle between egocentric desires would be replaced by working together toward community goals. Such benevolence would not be motivated by paternalism or guilt but would rise naturally from the realization that what humanely benefits the whole community benefits the individual and vice versa.

Because of our interdependence, individuals must consider the good of the community, and, at the same time, the community must keep in mind the good of the individual. With an attitude of interdependence, our goals and accomplishments would be viewed as much in terms of the community as ourselves.

Our interconnectedness extends worldwide. Just as no person is an island, no country can "go it alone." We are faced with obvious global interdependence especially considering the factors of instant communication, increasing population, depleted resources, and symbiotic trade. We also rely on each other to preserve the earth as the only home available to us. Once we realize this and accept that we *must* live and work together, we will begin to treat each other with respect and consideration. An interdependent world that realizes its interdependence would dismantle the threat of nuclear holocaust and do all possible to reverse the flood of ecological devastation.

We need to understand that the community is not just those persons we see everyday. The community of interdependence must include the whole earth. This means taking into consideration what our actions may do to others when we decide to use our earth for tilling, mining, manufacturing, and various kinds of developing. It also means realizing how we, in turn, are affected by the actions of others. The more we focus on the whole earth community, the more we will learn about it. The more we learn, the more we will care about other people and the earth in general.

Cooperation

One thing is certain: there will be no compassion as long as we continue to honor the god of competition.
—Matthew Fox

An attitude of interdependence can be expressed in two main ways: cooperation and responsibility. Cooperation is a logical result of, and is necessary for, interdependence. Whereas competition quickly undermines interdependence, cooperation nurtures and encourages it.

Cooperation literally means "working together." We suggest that it should also mean "creating together." Working together creatively is crucial in geo-communocentrism because working against each other or alone just doesn't make sense in an interdependent society. Whereas in competition only one person or group can win, in cooperation everyone can attain the goal desired, by working and creating together. Cooperation involves mediation, attempting to solve problems to the benefit of all. It means taking others into account, involving them in our decisions and goals.

The American tradition of town meetings is based on cooperation. In order to work effectively, democracy must operate through cooperation. When we compete, only the strongest win, only the strongest get heard. In cooperation we are all treated equally and given equal chance to express our views and shape our future.

As mentioned earlier, many believe that competition is necessary to motivate people to do bigger and better things. If we appreciate that our worth is immutable, we will understand that competing gains us nothing and it therefore will not serve as motivation. Seen from the intrinsic worth perspective, competition is a total waste of time and energy. With no need to gain or protect our sense of worth, there is no need to compete. Since we are interdependent there can be no separation between "winners" and "losers," and without such designations competition loses it meaning. Cooperation is much more useful and appropriate for people who realize their interdependence.

If we are guided by geo-communocentrism, motivation for improving our knowledge and skills comes not from trying to be better than someone else. Rather, learning is engaged in because of our natural curiosity. Athletic activity is pursued for its healthful benefits and because physical activity is basic to being human.

American society is not devoid of cooperation. Besides the tradition of cooperative, communal groups, we work together in various ways daily—carpools, division of labor, working through a disagreement with a loved one, taking our turn at four-way stops, and sharing toys in daycare centers. But these instances are few compared to the expressions of competition. However much we encourage our children to cooperate, however much we value the ideal, we have the feeling it just isn't practical. However, with a geo-communocentric worldview, cooperation would be a natural, logical way of relating. Instead of an unrealized ideal, cooperation would be a matter of course.

Because of our awareness of our interdependence, we would not perceive conflict as a situation where we must win and make someone else lose. It would be obvious that we all must "win" or no one does. Thus our "instinctive" response to conflict would not be digging holes, angry words, blows, or other competitive acts used to defend our worth. Knowing our worth were not threatened, we would be able to deal with the situation through discussion or mediation. Instead of fighting it out to see who could win the most, we would try to work things out to the benefit of all concerned. Such mediation would be as commonplace in families, labor disputes, board rooms, playgrounds, and international conflicts as arguments and threats are today.

Cooperation could also extend into government as more and more decisions could be made by town meetings or similar community forums. Questions about rezoning, expansion, and use of taxes could be decided cooperatively, with all being involved in the process. Education would also be enhanced by cooperation. Students could work together to solve problems and expand their knowledge, achieving much more than could be accomplished working against each other. Teachers could become guides, advisers, and resource persons instead of disciplinarians. This would encourage children to follow their natural curiosity and enthusiasm for learning. Just as children schooled in competition perpetuate econo-egocentrism, children skilled in cooperating would help create and develop a geo-communocentric society.

Responsibility

It all means, and sooner rather than later, that we who want to move beyond the present must commit ourselves to a new ethical system. The private gain and private pleasure of possessive individualism must give way to helping other people. Must give way, that is, to being citizens of a community.

—William A. Williams

Whereas cooperation is how we interact with others, responsibility is how we understand this connection with others. Responsibility also involves the relationship between the individual and the community.

Responsibility is too often understood to be the ability to fulfill a duty or obligation. But this is more accurately "dependability," obedience, or even subservience. Responsibility is a much more complicated matter.

Dietrich Bonhoeffer wrote of responsibility as being an interplay between freedom and obedience.[1] He said that to be responsible we must make decisions in such a manner that we are obedient to our freedom as individuals. We must never make decisions because of duty, the influence of another person, or a special set of circumstances. All these are to be considered, but should never be used as the reason or excuse for deciding one way or the other.

Bonhoeffer's ideas are well illustrated in the complementarity of the oriental yin/yang symbol. In the symbol, opposites are brought together into wholeness. There is something of each in the other. The one cannot be understood except in reference to the other. "Day" makes no sense unless there is some concept of "night." It is unreal to speak of "male" unless there is "female." There is no meaning to "cold" if there is no "hot." If we place "freedom" and "obedience" in the yin/yang model we can see that to say "freedom" with no sense of what it means to say "obedience" leaves us with license and anarchy. To say "obedience" with no sense of what it means to express our "freedom" leaves us with conformity and tyranny. The interdependence of freedom and obedience is the foundation of responsibility.

To be obedient to our own freedom, we must observe the circumstances, judge the various courses of action, weigh up the differing values, decide, and act out of our own freedom. In this way we do not give over our decisions to a principle, another person, or a particular circumstance. We will not say, "I decided to say that because honesty is the best policy"; or "I did it because my boss said I must"; or "The devil made me do it"; or "Everyone else was acting that way." We will able to say, "After due consideration of the information available, I decided my course of action. If it produces a positive effect, I decided. If it produces a negative effect, I decided. Whatever the outcome, I am responsible for my actions." In order to be responsible, we must be obedient to our own freedom to think and to choose. If we decide to follow the wishes of others, we consciously make that decision out of our own freedom to decide.

This method of deciding and acting allows no reliance on "expertism." We may be advised and informed by those with more experience and training in a certain area. But ultimately *we* make the decisions and are responsible for the outcome. Such open acceptance of responsibility would alleviate many of the problems that arise from finger-pointing, hidden agendas, and covert power plays. Making our own decisions and accepting the responsibility for the results enable us to be honest about our interests, respect the interests of others, and grow from our mistakes.

This balance between freedom and obedience underlies the relation between the individual and the community. At this level, responsibility may be called "civic virtue." We do not have to decide between license on one hand and conformity on the other, or between anarchy and slavery. In civic virtue there is give-and-take and the yin/yang sense that there must be interdependence between the individual and the community—neither can survive without the other.

The individual can act responsibly toward the community, taking into consideration how individual acts affect others and the good of the whole community. However, the community is also responsible to the individual, to make sure individual needs are taken into account, and valuing and respecting each person as an individual as well as part of the community. When this happens, the sense of isolation and alienation that so afflicts our world of extrinsic worth is no longer a problem.

Responsible interaction between an individual and a community of one hundred people may seem possible, but in a community of 50,000 it would surely offer more problems. This is certainly true in a society valuing competition, directive power, and the exclusionist attitude. However, if each person would respect and trust every other person in the community, such interaction would occur more naturally and smoothly. A "community" of 50,000 may not feel intimate and close, but each individual would not have to worry about his or her rights being ignored or violated.

We are certainly capable of responsible behavior, for even with the influence of econo-egocentrism we do act in accord with this notion of responsibility at times. An act as simple as picking up a tack so no one will step on it or throwing our trash in the trashcan instead of on the street are acts of responsibility — but only if we do so with a sense of interdependence. Such acts are *not* responsible if we perform them out of fear, guilt, or a sense of obligation.

We have set up agencies like United Way that help those who cannot survive on their own, or who have temporarily "fallen through the cracks." We have numerous regulatory and "watchdog" groups designed to keep an eye on government and industry for the good of the society. These groups attest to the lack of responsibility in our society, for they are needed only because our society does not encourage responsible behavior, practices, and decisions. If we were a responsible society, we would not need these regulatory groups. We would provide our own self-regulation through a heightened sense of responsibility.

Such a "natural" response could be expected if we held an attitude of interdependence and acted cooperatively. When we work together with the realization that we cannot separate ourselves from one another, taking the community into account comes naturally.

See below chapter 14, "Trying It on for Size," pages 133ff., nos. 25, 27, and 45.

See below chapter 15, "Food for Thought," pages 168ff., nos. 5, 20, 32, and 53.

CHAPTER 8

... And Its Possibilities

"Once the American people have seen the hazard of continuing the course we have been following, ... once they have sorted out their values" they "can be extraordinarily imaginative and resourceful ... in bringing their convictions to bear on both personal life-styles and public policy." —R. E. Miles, Jr.

Geo-communocentrism, as we have envisioned it, is thus based on the values of interdependence, cooperation, and responsibility. Worldviews, however, are complex and multi-faceted and cannot be described as simply three ways of relating. We must take our envisioning one step further and explore how these values would interact to influence our lives more fully. The resulting attitudes, understanding, and behaviors would necessarily be interconnected; each would influence and be influenced by the other. Through envisioning we can attempt to distinguish each thread of this complex web in order to begin to understand how a geo-communocentric ethic could influence our lives.

Dialogic Thinking

When we try to pick out anything by itself, we find it hitched to everything else in the Universe.
—John Muir

A dialogue is a process for the interchange and discussion of ideas in a manner that is open and frank. Its purpose is the seeking of understanding and harmony.

Dialogic thinking is the same process in the mind of an individual. Whereas dualistic thinking considers things only in terms of two opposite and possibly antagonistic factors, dialogic thinking seeks to understand things along a continuum, or to see various facets to a problem, or to appreciate more than two perspectives in any given situation.

People who are free from trying to protect their sense of worth are free to entertain such a variety of notions, ideas, and beliefs. They can host divergent thinking as well as convergent thinking. Instead of always feeling they must have "the" answer, they can be open to several answers. Unlike the blind men with the elephant, they can accept that more than one perception can be right.

Replacing dualistic thinking with dialogic thinking would mean profound changes in our thought processes, our creative ability, and, specifically, our attitude toward differences and conflicts. By allowing for variation and alternatives, dialogic thinking enables and encourages creativity. Realizing there are more than two sides to any situation allows us to look at it in its entirely from different viewpoints. This sort of creative inquiry and discovery paves the way for the development of new understanding.

By allowing for alternatives, dialogic thinking enables us to "be who we are" rather than fitting into one side or the other. Humans are a mass of maybes, inconsistencies, and "gray areas"; we don't fit into definite "black" or "white" categories. Dialogic thinking gives room for our complex nature. Free to express the intricacies of who we are, we gain a sense of social acceptance to go along with the "cosmic" acceptance found in the idea of intrinsic worth.

No longer would we see ourselves as "good" pitted against "evil." We would realize that we are people whose interests happen to conflict; we are interdependent people who can cooperate. This would be true for conflicts between the U.S. and the Soviet Union, labor and management, black people and white people, parents and children. If we see each other as merely different and not as antagonistic opposites, we can listen to the views of others, respect their needs, and expect them to do the same for us. This openness and respect would reduce tension within a family, between segments of the society, and among the nations of the world.

The openness and acceptance of dialogic thinking makes it difficult to divide ourselves between "us" and "them." We realize that issues and differences are much too complex for such myopic polarization. We feel no need to prove we are on the "right" side; therefore there is no one on the "wrong" side. There is no need to create divisions between us. We can relate to each other respectfully and inclusively.

Inclusionist Attitude

In our every deliberation, we must consider the impact of our decisions on the next seven generations...
—The Great Law of the Six Nations
Iroquois Confederacy

The inclusionist attitude holds that no one is better or worse than anyone else and therefore no one should be excluded from planning or celebrating or from having the necessities of life. It holds that we are indeed each different from the other but this does not mean we must be separate and antagonistic. We can value the differences and work together as equals. Since we all have the same worth, worth that cannot be increased or lost, we *are* equals. We may be different, but we are equals in terms of our significance.

No one is categorized as a member of "them," as opposed to "us." There is no need to label others as "losers," "turkeys," "nerds," "Gooks," or "Commies" because there is no need to dig holes for others in order to insure our worth. The inclusionist attitude extends to all people regardless of age, race, sex, nationality, sexual orientation, physical ability, or appearance. In the past, our differences have divided us all into "us" and "them." With no one having to gain some sense of worth by looking down on "them," we can realize that our differences are marvelous varieties that make the human species more colorful and interesting. We can value our differences just as we value the differences among birds or flowers. Our variations are to be wondered at and appreciated as a marvel of the universe.

Our interdependence extends beyond humanity and so can our sense of inclusion. We are interdependent with all other life forms and with the earth itself, therefore we include all life and the earth when we think of "us." All life has intrinsic worth; we cannot claim superiority over any living things. We are interdependent and equal. The inclusionist attitude also extends from the present into the past and the future. The past has given us the responsibility of celebrating our roots and remembering our heritage. And we must always keep the future in mind, for our children and grand-children will have to live with whatever we leave. In envisioning geo-communocentrism we are being inclusive, for we are creating new understandings that enable us to deal with the effects of the decisions we make today.

If the inclusionist attitude were to become predominant in our society, competition would decrease drastically. If we do not separate "us" and "them," we do not have the "sides" necessary for competition. Including everyone as "us" promotes cooperation, for it is only natural for "us" to work together.

An inclusionist attitude would guarantee the quintessential "equal opportunity" policy. *No one* would be automatically excluded; all are of equal worth and thus would be offered an equal chance at employment, housing, education. A pervasive attitude of inclusion would make "affirmative action" and other such policies obsolete. These policies are of utmost importance in an econo-egocentric society in the habit of excluding those who are different. With the realization that everyone has intrinsic worth, forced inclusion through rules, laws, and artificial incentives would not be necessary. Exclusion would seem unnatural. We would realize the injustice inherent in separating "them" from "us." Among those experiencing such realizations and attitude changes, discrimination and prejudice would be eliminated.

With an inclusionist attitude as part of the American world-view, democracy would be fortified and insured. In order to have a true democracy it must encompass the entire society. In American society, almost all are included in suffrage; we have political democracy to the extent that no one (over eighteen) is excluded from voting. However, because money is a determining factor in who can be elected to office and who carries the most influence and power in society, our "democracy" is not really inclusive.

An inclusionist attitude would also mean economic democracy, in which everyone would be included in the creation of economic policy and no one would be used as a pawn in the economic schemes of others.

If all were allowed equal economic and political inclusion, directive power would no longer be a viable method of dealing with conflict. The inclusionist attitude demands another definition and expression of "power." In geo-communocentrism power must encourage cooperation instead of competition and respect for the equality of all instead of the strength of the few. This is "synergic power."

Synergic Power

> *There are still moments when we see the processes of life continue to unfold, when we cannot help believing that life is moved by a power deeper than the power of the gun and the bomb; a power that might still prevail if we knew how to call it forth.* —Starhawk

Synergic power is *"the capacity of an individual or group to increase the satisfactions of all participants by intentionally generating increased energy and creativity."*[1] In other words, using synergic power means using our energy, talents, knowledge, and abilities to affect and influence the situation around us in order to co-create a more rewarding present and future for everyone.

Synergic power is not possible without a sense of interdependence, which enables us to see that helping ourselves includes helping others. Synergic power is not displayed in a conflict of strength to see who wins. Instead it is used cooperatively, in conjunction with others, to see how the situation can be worked out to the benefit of all. Thus, with synergic power there are no "sides" to be pitted against each other.

The equality of intrinsic worth and the inclusionist attitude does not mean that we would all be exactly alike. We would still have different talents, knowledge, and experiences to express and share. Such abilities offer a sort of "power," the power to change or create or heal or teach. They do not offer power over others. In synergic power, the important factor is that an ability offers power only if it is valued and utilized to the advantage of all. This attitude is possible only with an understanding of intrinsic worth. If we feel the need to gain worth wherever possible, we will use our talents and knowledge to our own advantage. With the security of intrinsic worth, we are free to share our abilities and use them cooperatively rather than competitively.

Synergic power thus enables creativity and cooperation. Unlike directive power, which decreases as more people try to wield it, synergic power increases as more and more are involved. We can combine our abilities and multiply our "power" rather than cancelling out each other's power through competition. Combining our power synergically, we can extend our creativity to change, improve, invent, and celebrate to a greater degree than we could manage on our own. Synergic power enables humans to realize more fully their creative potential.

Democracy

> *Every generation has to accomplish democracy over again for itself; . . . its very nature, its essence, is something that cannot be handed on from one person or one generation to another, but has to be worked out in terms of needs, problems and conditions of the social life of which, as the years go by, we are a part, a social life that is changing with extreme rapidity from year to year.*
> —John Dewey

Synergic power expressed in the governing of a society is called democracy. As we have seen, geo-communocentrism supports democracy through the inclusionist attitude, cooperation, and responsibility. But democracy can be seen as a facet of geo-communocentrism in and of itself. Just as the form of governance in econo-egocentrism is "expertism," governing in the geo-communocentric worldview is "democracy."

Democracy as "government of, by, and for the people" is based on, and is an expression of, geo-communocentric values. "Government *of* the people" means responsibility. A government of the people rather than of the experts depends on the responsibility of the people. To have government *of* the people we must accept the responsibility of making decisions ourselves and not leave it to the experts. To do so we must educate ourselves on the issues rather than acquiescing to what we are told. We must accept the results of our decisions; we are responsible whether it turns out well or not. Government *of* the people means *we* are responsible for our own governing.

Government *by* the people depends on cooperation. Government *by* the people means that all the people must be involved in the process of governing. For all to be involved we must cooperate, for when we compete only the strong have influence. Government *by* the people means *all* the people. Everyone's voice is heard, everyone's needs are considered—this is only possible through cooperation. Cooperation is the process of true democracy.

Government *for* the people is an expression of our interdependence. Government *for* the people means everyone should benefit. Because of our interdependence, if some of us are left out of the benefits of democracy, then none of us has experienced true democracy. We are all of worth, we are all part of one whole; we must all be empowered and free or no one is. Interdependence is the reason for democracy; government *for* the people means it is important that *everyone* is included in the freedom and empowerment of democracy.

Reverence Ethic

> *Reverential thinking pays homage to the interdependence of all forms of life. It seeks a harmony with nature. It stimulates a concern for maintenance and preservation, for working with rather than against nature.* — Daniel Yankelovich

One very important aspect of geo-communocentrism is the perspective it offers on our relationship to Creation: other people, fellow living things, the earth, the universe. In an ethic of intrinsic worth, Creation is perceived as wonderful and worthy in and of itself. As such it is to be regarded with reverence. Instead of the consumer ethic, geo-communocentrism offers an ethic of reverence.

The reverence ethic was manifested in the life and thought of Francis of Assisi. His vision prepares us for a "radically respectful life toward others and the created world."[2] His vision is "perfectly suited to an ecological recovery for a world scarred by insatiable 'wants.' Its value lies not in romantic notions of birds and nature, but of a steeled reverence for life, of taking only what is needed, and letting go of all the rest."[3]

To take more than our share is to fancy ourselves more important than our fellow human beings and other parts of Creation. To feel it is our right to use the earth in order to satisfy our econo-egocentric needs is to alienate ourselves from Creation, just as using other people alienates us from each other and prevents community.

In order to live, all life forms must rely on the death of other life forms, but only to the extent of what is needed to be healthy. When we decide that an animal or plant must die in order that we may eat or be free of disease or may have land for food, we must be aware of this fact of death, admit it, and be thankful for the portion of Creation that we use so that we might live. In this way we acknowledge our interdependence and remind ourselves that it is not our *right* but our *need* that allows us to cause these deaths. As a nation, we could have gained this understanding of the interrelatedness of all things years ago from the Native Americans, but our egocentrism prevented us from noticing or valuing this wisdom.

Many have called for a "responsible stewardship" through which we protect the environment as well as ourselves. There is trouble with this phrase, however, in that stewardship has the connotation of superiority, of being wiser than that over which we are stewards. Elizabeth Dodson Gray says the stewardship concept is "paternalistic, clothed still in hierarchical categories, and subtly related to such old ideas as 'enlightened slave owners' and 'the white man's burden.'" Such an approach tends to use directive power, which easily corrupts. "Self-interest always motivates those 'above' to the detriment of those 'below.' Great is the power of human rationalization to justify such self-interest and to make it appear 'responsible.'"[4]

The idea that we are "in charge of" Creation has led to mass exploitation and the loss of the pleasure of feeling part of "the natural world." This phrase itself is indicative of the econo-egocentric view of Creation. Saying "the natural world" sets it apart from "our world," creating a dualism of humans against nature. We ourselves are part of the natural world. We cannot work against it without working against ourselves.

We can cooperate with the earth and other living things just as we can with other people. We do so when we nurture the trees in an orchard and receive the fruit in return. We can work with Creation synergically and respectfully so that humans can have what they need without destroying the environment. Such symbiotic relationships are possible in most, if not all, our dealings with the "natural world."

The ethic of reverence towards Creation could pull us back from the brink of ecological disaster. We must realize that it may indeed be too late to reverse the process of ecological devastation. But we must try or give up hope, thus insuring destruction.

We may believe that it is impossible to save the environment without reverting to prehistoric living conditions. But survival need not signal the end of "civilization" as we know it. The widespread use of dialogic thinking, cooperation, and synergic power would be an excellent chance to produce creative ideas of new sources of power, food distribution, waste disposal, etc. There is more than enough food produced in the world now to feed everyone; greed, bureaucracy, and a lack of creativity prevent its equal distribution. We don't have to destroy the environment in order to maintain our society; we just have to cooperate, be creative, and come up with effective alternatives.

Secure in our worth, we would no longer need material wealth to prove and protect our worth. Stopping our ravenous consumerism, we would be able to live simply, celebrating the worth within that would no longer be lost under piles of extrinsic junk. A reverence ethic would call for re-prioritizing our values: *being* would be more important than *having,* life would be much more valued than wealth. We would no longer waste resources, decimate species, and despoil natural areas in the name of progress and our own materialistic egocentric needs.

The reverence ethic grows out of the idea that all parts of Creation have intrinsic worth and are thus of equal value. It is egalitarian rather than hierarchical, Creation-centered rather than focused only on human needs and desires. The reverence ethic includes justice and celebration and is the only attitude that makes sense in an interdependent Creation.

Respect and Dignity

> *If we truly honored the diversity in creation, we would move our culture to* a creation-based valuing of all parts of nature. *We would not place the value of any one species always above the others. All species would be validated by their basic imprimatur of worth given them in creation itself.*
>
> —Elizabeth Dodson Gray

As human beings, we like to think of ourselves as the most advanced and therefore the most significant parts of Creation. We are, however, made of the same kinds of subatomic particles and waves as everything else. All entities are conglomerations of the stuff of Creation; our specific conglomerations are no more significant than others. Everything is of equal importance and meaning. Every part of Creation is intrinsically worthy.

Realizing the basic equality and significance of all things leads to treating them with respect. We respect other people, pets, animals in the wild, trees, grass, flowers, bugs, and the earth itself because Creation has labored just as long to create them as it has to bring us into being. We respect all parts of Creation, including ourselves, because we are each unique and valuable parts of an interdependent Creation.

As such, we each have the dignity of being who we are. We need not view ourselves or any other parts of Creation as inherently imperfect or unimportant. We are who we have been created to be. A maple tree was created to be a maple tree. An alligator was created to be an alligator. A galaxy was created to be a galaxy. You were created to be you. We are each perfectly who we are; we each have the dignity of existence.

With this dignity comes the right to be as we have been created to be. We each have the right and should be accorded the respect to follow our own insights, meet our own needs, trust our own feelings, express our own uniqueness. We can share wisdom, experience, insight, support, and companionship, but no one can determine for another how he, she, or it *should* be.

This is, unfortunately, what econo-egocentrism has all too often caused us to do. We think the maple tree *should* be a chair. We think the alligator *should* be gotten rid of or made into a pair of shoes. We think the prairie *should* be a field of wheat. We think that the rabbit *should* be subject to our product and chemical testing. We think a river *should* wash away our wastes. This attitude is possible only if we view the tree, the rabbit, and the prairie as valuable only to the extent that they are useful to us.

This does not mean that we would never fell nor kill nor plow. We must do these things to some extent in order to survive. However, we would not be doing so from a misguided sense that our use of something is more worthwhile and important than its continued existence or the dignity of its own way of being. We would be acting out of our own dignity, out of our needs as living beings.

If Creation is regarded with reverence and we are part of Creation, we are to be held in reverence also. Each of us is a miracle to be valued and not wasted. This would mean increased respect for ourselves and others; we would be valued because we exist, not just because of the function we fill. We would relate to each other primarily as persons and only secondarily as roles, as we would not allow ourselves to be reduced to being mere cogs in a huge machine.

This sense of respect for our own dignity would not permit us to waste our time in activities we feel are meaningless and pleasureless. We have the right to be involved in meaningful, significant activity. "Honest work from which one can derive satisfaction (not simply a wage), a sense of working in a community with and for one's fellow men, and an opportunity to develop one's native talents for the benefit of self and others are just as important as income sufficient for a decent and dignified material existence."[5]

Respecting our dignity and realizing our need to be involved in significant activity would mean the revival of "real work": work that we enjoy, that eases suffering, or that produces a service or product that we feel really enhances life. This would mean focusing on the work itself rather than the work hours, emphasizing the service or product rather than the profit, and attempting to be involved in activity that is directly related to and meaningful for our personal lives.

We would be able to follow our vocation instead of just finding an occupation. An occupation is something that occupies our time. It provides a paycheck, but generally means little else to us. "Vocation" means calling. A vocation is something we feel called to do, something we really want to do, something we think is important and valuable in and of itself.

It's hard for us to think that we should enjoy what we do. Our society tells us that if you don't enjoy it you just grit your teeth and do it anyway. Your reward comes after five and on the weekends; that's when you do what you enjoy. This attitude does not respect who we are and does not recognize our dignity of existence. We have very valid feelings, insights, talents, and needs that we have every right to explore and express. Enjoying what we do is not being spoiled or irresponsible; it is expressing who we are. "Every man is called to give love to the work of his hands. Every man is called to be an artist."[6]

In our econo-egocentric society we often cannot follow our vocations because it is too hard to earn a living that way. It is hard to live on the income of a poet, a naturalist, or a pre-school teacher. A geo-communocentric society, aware of each person's intrinsic worth, would respect the dignity of our being who we have been called to be. If our inherent talents are to be a dancer or a clown, a doctor or a teacher of handicapped children, we could follow these vocations without being blocked by societal expectations or structures. Free from the hierarchical, exclusionist, competitive thinking of econo-egocentrism we would realize that such activities are worthwhile and worth supporting. Those people who usually have to volunteer their spare time to follow their vocations could be subsidized by those who value their efforts. A government of, by, and for people who value beauty, laughter, talent, health, compassion, and creative education would reprioritize our use of tax money. We could support a huge number of artists, clowns, nurses, teachers, and ombudspersons with the money it takes to build and maintain one nuclear submarine.

Recognizing the dignity of each of us and respecting our need for and right to have real, meaningful work would mean that we would have more workshops and fewer factories. We would become more self-sufficient and would make things of quality because we cared about the process as well as the product. We would have more painting, *creative* writing, and clowning; more weaving, exploring, inventing, legend-telling; more dancing, nature conserving, small farming, and massaging. We would have the chance to experience the joy of being involved in real work in which we can celebrate and "discover who we are, assume responsibility for ourselves and others, and lay the foundations for our own and society's future."[7]

See below chapter 14, "Trying It on for Size," pages 133ff., nos. 13, 26, 28, and 60.

See below chapter 15, "Food for Thought," below pages 168ff., nos. 13, 25, 48, 60.

CHAPTER 9

A Broader Definition of Religion

"Religare": *to bind again, to make whole.*

As we noted at the start of chapter 7, geo-communocentrism sounds utopian and hopelessly idealistic if understood in terms of the econo-egocentric worldview. Because such a perspective is dependent upon the notion of extrinsic worth, it is irrelevant in judging what would be possible if we acted on the idea of intrinsic worth instead. While laboring under the idea of extrinsic worth, it is easy to condemn these possibilities as ridiculous: "No one will ever do that," "What's in it for them?" "Nice idea, but impossible." But it is this very attitude that insures that econo-egocentrism will continue. The greatest obstacle to developing a worldview such as the one just suggested is the belief that it is impossible, that extrinsic worth is a universal truth, that there is no other way.

Of course, it is no surprise that we are so convinced of the validity of extrinsic worth: we've very rarely been offered an alternative. Christianity, as we have seen, could offer an alternative attitude toward human worth, but the churches have not been a loud voice of opposition to the dominant worldview. In fact, they have been very effective in their support of the idea of extrinsic worth and the econo-egocentric worldview.

Econo-egocentrism has in fact undermined the mission of the churches, subtly altering the message of Christianity for its own needs and goals. This has been possible because of the deeply-rooted function econo-egocentrism has played in our heritage. A worldview, as the understanding of how life is and how we relate to it, is by definition pervasive in a society. By affecting our deeply felt emotions and morals, econo-egocentrism has been able to inspire the strength of feeling and conviction associated with religion. Econo-egocentrism does indeed serve the function of a religion for us and for our society.

If we continue to define religion as solely a ritualized expression of belief in a divine or supernatural being, then econo-egocentrism's religious role will remain vague and misunderstood. What is needed is a broader definition of religion, one that takes into account contemporary anthropological, psychological, and sociological, as well as theological understandings. Attempts to redefine religion in this way have been made over the last several years.

W. A. Williams, historian, says "to be religious... means to acknowledge and to do one's very best to honor and practice a system of values. Such a structure of ideals may or may not invoke the name of God in the biblical sense, but it must provide *some* injunction to do certain things and not to do other things."[1]

For Erich Fromm, psychoanalyst, religion "does not refer to a system that has necessarily to do with a concept of God or with idols or even to a system perceived as religion, but to *any group-shared system of thought and action that offers the individual a frame of orientation and an object of devotion.*"[2]

H. Richard Niebuhr, theologian, says that religion consists of two factors: a center of value by which we come to understand ourselves, and loyalty to a cause that flows from that center of value and motivates our decisions in life. If we call the foci of the centers of value and loyalty "gods," then atheism does not exist. "To deny the reality of a supernatural being called God is one thing; to live without confidence in some center of value and without loyalty to a cause is another."[3]

Joseph Mathews, theologian, said that in order to be a self, a person has to have a god. That is, in order for us to have a sense of identity, we must have something over against which to understand ourselves, even if it is no more than the opinion of certain persons in our life.

By these definitions, religion is not confined to ritualized ceremonies, belief in a divine being, or membership in a religious organization. A religion is that which fulfills certain vital psychological and sociological needs — whether it is recognized as a religion or not. Thus *everyone* has a religion (regardless of what we claim) because we all must have something in our lives that fills these needs.

Two Functions of Religion

Every functioning society has, to an important degree, a common religion. The possession of a common set of ideas, rituals, and symbols can supply an overarching sense of unity even in a society otherwise riddled with conflicts. —Robin Williams

Religion has two basic functions that concern us here: personal and social. The personal function is to provide a personal system of values and beliefs, a frame of orientation, and a sense of identity in the midst of Creation. This function may be performed by an institutional religion, a recognized personal spirituality or philosophy, or anything in our lives that, consciously or unconsciously, gives meaning and structure to our existence.

The social function of religion is to offer a group-shared system of values and beliefs, to sacralize the traditions and goals of the community, and to provide a sense of group identity that bonds the members together. This function may be performed by an organized, metaphysical religion, a sense of heritage and tradition, devotion to a goal, loyalty to a leader or an ideal, or even a sense of love and devotion to each other. Every social group, from a family to a nation to a world religious community, must have something that plays this role. Without this bonding force, there is nothing to keep the group together.

To understand the functions of religion we must look beyond what is usually labelled "religion" and discover what really fills these personal and social functions. When we do so, we realize that religion is much more pervasive in our lives than we usually believe.

In American society we like to compartmentalize our activities. We have a political life, an economic life, a family life, an educational life, and a religious life. Because these "lives" are carried on in different social institutions, we often believe that they are not, and often should not be, connected with or influence each other. In this fragmented view of life, "religion" refers only to our organized, metaphysical religions.

Homogeneous, tribal societies of the past did not hold such a compartmentalized view. For such people there was no way of dividing the religious from other parts of life. All were seen as parts of the whole, parts of what it meant to be human and a member of the society. There was one system of values and beliefs that was pervasive of the entire life of the society. Each act was part of what gave identity and meaning or what bonded the group together. When a member of a tribe made a pot or a spear or went on a hunt or told a story at the fire, that person was acting religiously. With every action, the members of the tribe were constantly manifesting and expressing the tribe's understanding of what made life significant.

Religion was just as pervasive in homogeneous, urban societies in the ancient world. In those situations, "the state and religion were so completely identified it was impossible even to distinguish one from the other.... Every city had its city religion; a city was a little church all complete with its gods, its dogmas, and its worship."[4] Socrates came to his death because he was perceived as a threat to the civic religion of Athens.

In Mesopotamia, the city-state was an estate or manor owned and run by the city god. The city-state's role was to "provide the god with the essentials of life: food, clothing, and shelter."[5] The roles of the inhabitants were to be "sharecroppers, serfs or servants of the gods"; their lives and everything they did had significance only in terms of this religious role.[6]

This pervasive, ubiquitous sort of religion worked, however, only as long as the societies remained homogeneous and relatively stable. As world population increased and travel, trade, and conquest became more frequent, societies began to lose their homogeneous nature. No longer was there one religion, one god or set of gods, one common history to give the society a sense of identity and purpose. Such a pluralistic society, however, had to have something to bond the people together, to establish some kind of order, and to provide a sense of community.

The one, all-pervasive, tribal religion was no longer functional as a bonding force for the society. The various metaphysical religions were, instead, potentially divisive in the community. The bonding function of religion had to be filled in some other way. Since what all people in the society had in common was the society itself, the social function of religion came to be filled by the political body. The state came to develop its own system of values, beliefs, and identity that was separate from that of the metaphysical religions. This system was shared by all in the society and thus served the bonding function of religion.

Though this "bonding religion" and the metaphysical religions were separate and distinct, they had to be compatible. They had to share a basic understanding of life, fundamental social values, and a willingness to allow each other their own sphere of influence. If this were not the case, the opposing values and loyalties would be divisive and possibly cause the disintegration of the society.

The balance between the two sorts of religion is well illustrated in the case of ancient Rome. The bonding religion was a formally organized religion; "the Roman state cult under the emperors served as the civil religion of the realm. Various particular religions existed alongside it, and their adherents could practice as enthusiastically as they pleased as long as they gave nominal acceptance to the state cult. But this nominal acceptance was obligatory."[7]

The refusal by Christians to participate in the rites of the civil religion was not seen by the Romans as a theological problem, but as a political one. To keep the vast empire together, the leaders felt they needed a binding factor that would give the people a sense of common identity. Christians refused to give loyalty to anything other than their God and thus were seen as a challenge to the state religion's authority in the political and social arena.

Christianity and the Roman state religion did not share basic values or a similar understanding of life. They disagreed about their rightful spheres of influence. The use of the concept "Kingdom" by the Christians, not surprisingly, threatened the Roman leadership. The two religions were not compatible and this division threatened the structure and cohesion of the society. The tension was not resolved until Christianity itself became the state religion under the reign of Constantine in the fourth century.

Individuals, and thus groups of individuals, cannot live according to two conflicting systems of values and beliefs. Where two such systems exist, either the society will break up or the systems will adjust themselves to each other until they are compatible. One of the systems may disintegrate in the face of the strength of the other. One might force the other to change its general understanding to be compatible. Or there might be compromise, a give and take of values between the two. However it occurs, the end result must be a general, basic compatibility or the society cannot hold together.

Thus, the condition of religion in pluralistic societies is actually not very different from the situation in homogeneous societies. In either one there must be one system of values and beliefs that is pervasive in the society. The difference is that in a pluralistic society the social function and the personal function are carried out by separate social institutions. The outer expressions of the bonding religion and the metaphysical religions may be very different and may even conflict, but the underlying values and ethics must be basically the same.

Hidden Religion

> *Religion is those feelings, symbols, and acts that bind a group together; and since there are many groups, there are many "religions." A person can be a member of many at one and the same time.*
>
> —Herbert Richardson

Such "layering" of religions occurs on the personal level as well. We may claim any of several metaphysical religions as our own. As part of the society, however, we will be influenced by the underlying system of values of the bonding religion regardless of whether these values are compatible with those of our chosen religion.

Since this underlying system usually goes unrecognized or unstated and is often masked by a person's stated religion, it can be referred to as the "hidden religion." What we *profess* is our stated, institutional religion. What we actually *do* is based on our real, though possibly hidden, religion. These may indeed be the same, but more often they are not: "Often... individuals are not even aware of the real objects of their personal devotion and mistake their 'official' beliefs for their real, though *secret* religion. If, for instance, a man worships power while professing a religion of love, the religion of power is his secret religion while his so-called official religion, for example, Christianity, is only an ideology."[8]

Whether a religion holds real power for a person or is just given lip-service can be determined by the person's actions. Beliefs and values, like trees, can be recognized by the fruit they bear. Someone who professes a religion of love while unconsciously worshipping power will most often make important decisions based on power instead of love. To determine what we really value, what our true religion is, we must look very closely at what we *do* rather than at what we *say.*

A very blatant example of this is the long and bloody history of warfare between ostensibly Christian nations. For almost two thousand years, Christian leaders, claiming allegiance to the Prince of Peace, have waged war after war against other Christian leaders. The values behind such actions could not possibly be those of forgiveness and loving kindness. It would seem more likely that the motivations have been pride, greed, and exclusionism.

Observers of Latin American cultures maintain that although Roman Catholicism is the stated religion of the vast majority of the people with Indian background, often the real though hidden religion is tribal. The value systems have not been changed; rather the names of the gods have been changed to the names of the saints. What results is a fascinating blend of the two traditions. This blend is nominally Christian, but much of its power and the loyalty it claims is of the older tradition.

The point is not to debate the merits of patriotism, xenophobia, or tribal mythology. It is to indicate that what people claim to be their religion may not be their real religion at all. What we say and what we do are often different.

In the U.S. many people profess to be Christian. By looking at individual decisions and our decisions as a society, however, it becomes apparent that we do not often act on the values of Christianity. We do not act on generosity, compassion, simplicity, and loving kindness nearly as much as we act on greed, competition, materialism, and defensive antagonism. What we are acting upon is our hidden religion — econo-egocentrism.

Officially we have no state religion. There are no state ordained worship services, no official creed or doctrine, and we don't have to prove officially that we are "true believers" in order to be accepted as citizens. Econo-egocentrism, however, does make analogous demands; their religious aspects are just more subtle. Millions of us attend various kinds of competitions with fervent devotion. Saluting the flag and reciting the pledge of allegiance are expected and enforced, socially if not legally. Anyone who does not conform to our way of life, or who criticizes America, is told to "shape up or ship out." Bumper stickers that proclaim, "America, love it or leave it," and "'I believe in America" can be understood as religious statements of our bonding religion. If actions can reveal the hidden religion for nations as well as for individuals, then a close look at American society reveals that econo-egocentrism is our bonding religion, our unstated state religion.

See below chapter 15, "Food for Thought," pages 168ff., no. 36.

CHAPTER 10

Yankee Doodle Doctrine

There is nothing the church (or anyone else) believes that cannot be woven into the state's mythology.
—Herbert Richardson

Judging by our actions through the years, both domestically and internationally, it should be evident that econo-egocentrism has been our bonding religion throughout the history of our country. Again and again we have loyally acted in accordance with the values of this worldview, though these actions often ran counter to our professed metaphysical religions.

Slavery was obviously antithetical to the belief that all people are children of God. But it continued as a common practice, even among Christian landowners. It gave them the advantage of cheap labor in economic competition plus it provided someone for them to look down on. The forcible removal or eradication of Native American tribes so that land could be available for selling and buying has been going on for 350 years. This was done not on the basis that "all men are created equal," but on the competitive boast that "to the victor belong the spoils." And the huddled masses that came to this country yearning to breathe free continued to huddle together in ethnic ghettos until they found ways of conforming to the economic structures. Not until they were economically productive did they find full inclusion in the political system.

In foreign relations, we have repeatedly supported dictators with horrible human rights records because they were friendly to American "interests." Though we would claim otherwise, our actions show that these interests (read "economic gain") have seemed more important to us than the self-determination, democratic liberty, and the survival of the poor and powerless in other countries.

Priesthood

The ordained economic hierarchy who advise presidents represent an elite that has failed utterly in imagining basic solutions to the real economic realities of unemployment, violent employment, grotesque distribution, wealth, racism, sexism, inflation and competitive violence built into our economic system.

—Matthew Fox

Any religion has its "priests," its trained clergy who lead the lay people through the complexities of the religion. Priests are generally honored persons, holders of the sacred knowledge, who interpret and teach this knowledge, preside over and direct rituals, and encourage the faith.

In econo-egocentrism, these are the economists, the upper-echelon bureaucrats, the corporate managers, the politicians. They are "a special class of experts in charge of our survival and well-being, 'a priesthood of... technologists.'"[1]

These priests thrive on expertism. Designated as experts by their graduate degrees, high-status jobs, or their own claims, these technocrats hold the "sacred" knowledge and thus call on us to trust them with decisions that affect our lives.

A role of priesthood is to interpret and teach knowledge, but it is up to the priests to determine how much of the knowledge is shared. Purposely or not, we are kept in the dark by the use of overly technical explanations, tax forms, bureaucratic language, and disclaimers that the matter is too confusing for the public to understand. The technocratic priests would lose some of their mystique and power if these documents were written in the vernacular. As it is we are so confused that we are willing to let the experts make the decisions.

Toffler says that technocrats suffer from tunnel-vision and tend to be myopic, thinking about "immediate returns, immediate consequences."[2] These priests are afflicted by what he calls "econothink." "Except during war and dire emergency, they start from the premise that even non-economic problems can be solved with economic remedies."[3]

Mission/Witness

It is our Manifest Destiny to overspread and to possess the whole of the continent which Providence has given us for the development of the great experiment of liberty and federative self-government entrusted to us.
—John L. O'Sullivan, 1845

Like Christianity, econo-egocentrism has a mission to spread the "word" and to proselytize for new adherents. The mission of econo-egocentrism has always had a messianic quality as we have sought to influence the rest of the world to think and do as we. One of the oldest images we have of ourselves, as we saw above, is "the City upon a Hill." The Puritan colony was to be a model community for all the world to see. It was often spoken of as the "New Israel" chosen by God to lead all others to the understanding of what community at its best could be. The independence movement, when it had achieved success, stressed the idea that the U.S. should be the leader that would bring the world to freedom. A sense of mission developed and a strong tendency to shape the world in our image blossomed in the thinking of the citizenry.

For Americans to export a message of political democracy was idealistic at best. The American democratic experiment was based on a long heritage of English common law and parliamentary institutions. Few other nations shared such a tradition, and thus our particular version of democracy was inappropriate for their situations. However great this problem, it was not that which doomed the evangelical effort to failure. What went wrong was that the symbols of liberty were used by citizens and government alike to legitimate our fascination with buying and selling. "Liberty" was seen as the opportunity to pursue one's own interests free from interference by government or anyone else. "Liberty" was interpreted as laissez-faire economics.

It became our "manifest destiny" to extend our frontiers "from sea to sea and from Panama to the Pole." Where we could not extend direct political control we extended strong economic influence. This was not an attempt at empire, although economic empire resulted, but an expression of what was truly felt to be America's role in the world.

For various economic and political reasons, including their own national pride, other nations often could not or would not adapt their ways to the ways of the U.S. Their failure to do so was sometimes perceived in this country as an insult and some would call for a more vigorous crusade to influence them to be as we wanted them to be. Few paid attention to John Quincy Adams, who said that the "propensity to crusade was the 'most pernicious tendency' among Americans." He warned that "indulging in that penchant would 'change the very foundations of our own government from *liberty* to *power.*' " It would appear that his prediction was well-founded.[4]

Religious Training

School is an advertising agency which makes you believe you need society the way it is.

—Ivan Illich

All religions train their young in the beliefs and mores of the religion. Training is the only aspect of our bonding religion to have a formal institution through which it is expressed: the schools.

Almost everyone would agree that the purpose of the schools is to educate our children. Why such an education is important, however, and thus what should be taught, are subjects for continuing discussion. A democracy demands a well-informed electorate; thus an important reason for education is to train citizens to enter effectively into the democratic process.

But if you ask almost any student in junior high or above why he or she is in school, the answer will have to do with getting a good job. Students rarely talk about going to school to learn how to participate responsibly in a democratic society. They hear very few teachers, administrators, or parents speaking in such a way. What they do hear from their elders is that students should be able to support themselves when they get through the schooling process. We know of one guidance counselor who annually addressed the seventh and eighth graders before him with, "Kids, the name of the game is job-getting!"

For a hundred years, at least, the schools have been used as a socializing agent that (*a*) trains the young in qualities deemed best suited for their participation in the economic system, and (*b*) sorts each generation according to identified talents that meet the needs of the economy. Ivan Illich, introducing Joel Springs's argument in *Education and the Rise of the Corporate State,* says, "The primary purpose of the school system is social control for a corporate state, and for an economy which has as its goal the efficient production and the disciplined consumption of growing amounts of goods and services."[5] In like manner, Pirages and Ehrlich maintain, "The school system is now clearly a vast complex apparatus for transmitting the DSP" (dominant social paradigm).[6] What is transmitted is the importance of egocentrism, competition, conformity, expertism, and all the other factors of econo-egocentrism.

Very little training is received in schools on how to participate in a democratic society. One can hardly find training on how to be a responsible committee member. Student governments have "never provided training in the exercise of power but only in the mechanical details."[7] What power student governments have had has been termed "play-pen" power. Students may make decisions, but only in limited and watched-over areas such as homecoming festivities, proms, or money-raising activities for the school. All this takes place under the watchfulness of the administration and usually without any real issues discussed. Even the Supreme Court has agreed, in the school newspaper decision of 1987, that the students should learn the procedural methods of democracy but not the responsibility and freedom that goes along with it. "Democracy" is seen as a way of maintaining "effective social order" within the school and giving the students a chance to agree with the administrators.[8]

Fear of failure is a prime element in the lifestyle of many schools. This fear is utilized to train students to learn how to be taught rather than learn how to learn. Learning to learn involves risk and the threat of failure. Learning to be taught involves following what the teacher or textbook says. In order to survive the competition, the student must believe, at least for school purposes, that the teacher knows best. "In order not to fail most students are willing to believe anything and to care not whether what they are told is true or false. Thus one becomes absurd by being afraid; but paradoxically *only by remaining absurd can one feel free from fear.*"[9]

In order that all children be well-schooled, none may be allowed to absent themselves from the training. Schooling, therefore, must be compulsory. "We require kids to stay in school until they are 16 or so in order to make them into what we need them to be."[10] Thus their options do not include finding out what *they* need or want to be. Their options are determined, for the most part, by "what are you going to be?" which translates as, "how are you going to fit into the economic system?"

What offended so many Americans about the "hippies" of the 1960s was not their use of drugs, but their refusal to be what the economy needed them to be. Many "yuppies" of the 1980s used drugs, but they fit our idea of what enterprising young people should be. Therefore, they were not threatening.

The schools are charged with making sure that each generation understands and appreciates the econo-egocentric values and priorities: punctuality, conformity, competition, consuming. They also serve to instill attitudes of economic and political utility such as "math-is-better-than-music" and courses such as mechanics or business are more "practical" than poetry or ethics. One need only compare the job opportunities and starting salaries of those who graduate with engineering or business degrees and those who earn B.A.'s in literature or history to see what is most highly valued.

One does not need to be well-educated, but *must* be well-schooled, to be a proper devotee of econo-egocentrism. Since the schools function not unlike a state church for the national religion, it might be said, as of old, "extra ecclesiam, nulla salus" ("outside the church there is no salvation").[11] Only through proper schooling can we make something of ourselves, fit into the economic system, and therefore be of worth.

Worship

> *As [Todd] Gitlin has observed, television shows us people who are, above all, consumed by ambition and the fear of ending up losers.* —Robert Bellah, et al.

Worship, in any religion, is the re-hearing of who the devotees understand themselves to be according to the values of the religion. Worship, in econo-egocentrism, reminds us that meaning lies in competition, conformity, and egocentrism.

Traditionally the tallest structures in a society are religious structures: the totem pole, the steeple, the temple, the minaret, the Gothic cathedral. In our society the tallest structures are the office buildings and the even taller television towers, what goes on in the former determining what comes out of the latter.[12]

There is hardly a home in the U.S. that does not have one or more TV sets. The set occupies a place in the home not unlike a shrine. People gather before it and hear the word of "salvation." This message of salvation is expressed in seemingly infinite variations of the having formula: "If you buy ______, then you will be able to ______." The blanks are filled in by the particular advertiser. The saving word says that by purchasing a particular product the individual will be happier, sexier, or more secure in his or her quest to be "somebody." Children are not excluded from this means of worship. Future devotees are trained with the words: "Be the first on your block to have a ______."

The content of TV programming is a constant stream of various forms of competition. Large numbers of worshipers gather for the high holidays of the World Series and the Super Bowl. The soap operas, sitcoms, movies, game shows, and children's cartoons all stress competition. Though they probably do not realize it, those who sit and watch by the hour participate in econo-egocentric worship. They are re-hearing who they understand themselves to be, and who the society understands them to be, as conforming, competing consumers.

In the econo-egocentrism of the past, the act of working was a form of worship because it was through work that the free enterprise system was maintained and it, in turn, brought money or some other form of wealth. Today, consuming can be considered an act of worship because it keeps the economy going and reminds us of the values we hold to be true within the econo-egocentric frame of understanding. Thus, one of the main ways we celebrate holidays such as Presidents' Day, Memorial Day, Father's and Mother's Days, the Fourth of July, and Labor Day is with "special sales" — a ritual in which everyone is encouraged to participate.

Symbol and myth and worship all come together at national events such as the Bicentennial Year of 1976 and the Centennial of the Statue of Liberty in 1986. Anything that could remotely be connected to these events was manufactured and sold. The way to celebrate (worship) the 200th birthday of our nation-state was to purchase a flag, a statue of Benjamin Franklin, a red, white, and blue toilet seat cover, or pancake syrup in old-fashioned bottles. In this effort, dubbed by some the "buy-centennial," there was the chance to use some of the images and symbols most closely associated with the first tradition. This was done to legitimate the sale of what was, for the most part, ill-conceived and ill-made junk.

This didn't matter to many who bought, for buying in itself is one of the key methods of celebrating who we understand ourselves to be as a nation.

In 1984, the president, the sports establishment, the media, and millions of citizens turned an event that was ostensibly international into an extended econo-egocentric worship service. The Olympic Games, held in Los Angeles, spawned hundreds of "official" products and hundreds of millions of dollars were spent on advertising. Somehow the carrying of the torch across the United States became a patriotic endeavor; what was supposed to be a symbol of international cooperation was hailed as a nationalistic triumph. Whether it would have been this way if the Eastern bloc countries had been present we will never know. But as it was, our egocentrism was fully displayed during the expressions of nationalism and our econocentrism was evident during the commercials.

Through "worship services" like these, we remind ourselves of who we are and what we believe in. We are "Number 1," and therefore we have worth. We are the greatest nation in the world; thus, as citizens, each of us has significance. We believe that claiming and protecting that significance are the most important things we can do. To this end we believe in the ultimate value of competition and the importance of subtle, but definite conformity. We may not openly attest to these beliefs, but as a nation and as individuals, we act on them. These are the values that give us a sense of identity.

See below chapter 15, "Food for Thought," pages 168ff., nos. 4, 18, 31, and 63.

CHAPTER 11

The Subversion of the Good News

> *The churches have been wholly caught up in the American success story. They have travelled the exhilarating journey by the same routes as the rest of the nation.... The churches have in fact provided religious sanction for the cultural creed. They have given a materially self-indulgent way of life one benediction upon another, despite occasional protestations. Minority exceptions have existed but they have been just that — minorities and exceptions.*
>
> — Bruce Birch and Larry Rasmussen

Econo-egocentrism not only created its own rituals of worship, it usurped those of Christianity as well. Through the use of Christian symbols and rituals, econo-egocentrism legitimated itself as a religion. The identity with Christianity also concretized the power, appeal, and validity of the worldview. "The rituals of [the] older religion were transformed into the ceremonies of nationalism, and...these in turn influence men to deepen their worship [of nationalism]."[1]

Throughout U.S. history, biblical imagery has been applied to events, ideals, and important persons. Images of Washington as a Moses and Lincoln as a Christ-figure were popular at certain times.[2] The "wilderness" experience, the "City upon a Hill," the "American Israel," the idea of the promised land "flowing with milk and honey" were all used to try to describe the American experience.

The new nation was seen as God's chosen people. Many leading politicians minced no words in expressing their belief in America's divine sanction. Andrew Jackson once said that God "had charged the United States with the unique responsibility of preserving freedom 'for the benefit of the human race.'"[3] Lincoln's secretary of state, William Seward, referred to America as a "new and further development of the Christian system."[4] In later years this sentiment has not been expressed quite so blatantly, but it is still there, especially when the speakers are attacking "Godless Communism." The attitude is expressed in a popular bumper sticker that reads, "God, guns, and guts made America; let's keep all three!"

In a study on the inculcation of nationalism in the schools of the United States from 1776 to 1885, 800 textbooks were surveyed. It was found that the purposes and ideals of American nationalism were often identified with Christianity: "The United States is a Protestant nation with a divinely appointed mission. As the modern Chosen People its inhabitants have a special motive for patriotism. American nationalism and religion are thoroughly interwoven; love of the American nation is a correlative of love of God."[5] Over the past century, what we teach school children about nationalism has become less dogmatic, but it has remained an important part of the curriculum.

With such beliefs it is not surprising that Americans have had a tendency to use the word "God" to legitimate political and economic actions. "God in all his many forms has been invoked in every American confrontation with the world.... The 'licentious' French, the Black Catholics of Latin America, the infidels of Turkey, Islam and Asia, and the atheistic Reds of modern times."[6] The word "God" has been used to legitimate slavery, genocide of Native Americans, and U.S. expansion abroad. Almost never is the word used consciously to distort Christian purposes. Rather these are unthinkingly assumed to be the same as our political and economic goals.

In the same manner, American nationalism is often unthinkingly assumed to be the same as Christian ideals and purposes. Figuratively, the churches have hoisted the American flag to the top of the steeples, much as the flags of conquerors are raised over captured ships and forts to indicate who now rules. Many churches place the American flag in the front of the sanctuary, often taking a place of honor. Many congregations include the Star Spangled Banner in their hymnals and hold special services for Independence Day Sunday. This is not necessarily wrong, but we should not assume that such symbols are a natural part of Christianity.

Many Americans feel that the church should "stay out of politics." This doesn't usually mean removing the flag or national anthem from church services. Rather it refers to criticism of the government. Draft resistance, the sanctuary movement, protest against nuclear weapons and defense spending, criticism of U.S. economic policy, and other expressions of political ideals are becoming more and more frequent among Christian groups and denominations. But even though these actions may arise from religious beliefs, many other church groups consider them inappropriately critical of America and therefore counter to what they feel are Christian ideals and purposes. Supporting our nation and its government is expected; most mainstream congregations have a vague belief that their ministry is somehow connected to the political goals of the U.S. It is often not realized that complacently supporting the government or even remaining silent on the issues is influencing public opinion and is therefore involvement in politics.

Econo-egocentrism in the Churches

> *The church has gone the way of its culture. Surrounded by affluence, it has let itself slide into a very affluent lifestyle, sometimes even arguing that this is the only way in which it will be taken seriously.*
>
> —Adam Finnerty

Through the identification of American ideals and Christianity, the values of econo-egocentrism have become the determining values in many American churches. Competition, conformity, and egocentrism influence the work and message of many churches to a surprising degree, especially considering how antithetical such values are to the gospel message of intrinsic worth.

Competition appears in the churches as they vie with each other in membership drives, often posting how many members they have like so many hamburgers sold. It also emerges in comparing church buildings or budgets or pipe organs or choirs. It shows up in the ubiquitous sports leagues and in the hierarchical struggle for control that goes on in many committees. Some churches even resort to competition between Sunday school classes to see who can raise the most money for the needy.

Conformity is a strong theme in almost all our churches. Many congregations are fairly homogeneous in terms of race, schooling, and economic class. This occurs because people join a church where they feel comfortable. The controversies and conflicts that would arise with diversity are thus avoided, but so is the spiritual growth that could result from sharing such varied experiences and viewpoints.

Conformity is clearly expressed in "Sunday clothes." Members conform to the fashion standard and expectations of the particular congregation. The person who arrives in jeans and a T-shirt or who dresses "too gaudy" for a worship service may not be openly reprimanded, but there will often be murmurs and questioning looks.

Though social conformity is widespread in the churches, it is the conformity of belief that is critical. All churches have certain requirements for membership — but at times these requirements are taken to an extreme. The beliefs of the congregation or denomination are felt to be the "one true way" and all must believe similarly — or be wrong. In extreme cases of dualistic thinking, any alternative beliefs or opinions are looked upon as the work of Satan.

Conformity often extends beyond religious creed to all parts of life. "You not only must think like us, you must also live, look, and love like us" is a common, though often unspoken, attitude in congregations caught in the extrinsic worth trap. This is dualism and the exclusionist attitude at work in institutional religion. This supposedly divine enforcement of conformity has been used to exclude a wide variety of people, including homosexuals, Communists, unwed mothers, and racial minorities. At one university run by a religious group, overweight students were required to lose weight in order to attend.

This sort of extreme rigidity often leads to severe guilt. If there is only one right way to behave, any deviance from that way must be wrong. Many church members have revealed that such beliefs led them to hate themselves whenever they could not meet the specifications. Recently a support network has formed to try to help such people recover a sense of self-esteem and freedom.

Egocentrism has also created misunderstanding and even antagonism between different congregations, sects, and denominations. Suffering from dualistic thinking and exclusionism, many church members often feel that those with different beliefs do not do things right and are therefore not as deserving of God's love.

The exclusionism and the distance increase when dealing with other religions. American Christians have often viewed other religions with disdain, distrust, and even hostility. In our supposedly open and accepting society there has been a recent and alarming growth in "churches" that profess neo-Nazism. Ku Klux Klan members almost exclusively profess to be Christian. Those who want to bring metaphysical religion back into the schools don't mean *any* religion. In practice, prayer in the schools means Christian prayer, excluding and disrespecting children of other religious backgrounds.

Theological Perversion

> *The popular theme that God blesses and serves America has been accompanied by no demand that Americans first of all serve God, or make any real sacrifice. And such popular religion is positively dangerous because it confirms the national complacency and self-righteousness at a time of world crisis. . . .*
>
> —H. J. Muller

Econo-egocentrism reinforces the idea that God's love is conditional and that therefore a person must do certain things and refrain from doing other things in order to prove worthy of God's love. No matter how much is said about God's steadfast love lasting forever, or God loving us even though we are sinners, our training in econo-egocentrism blocks our hearing the message.

God's "unconditional" love is all too often understood to be *only* for those who meet certain conditions. From such a perspective, God's love is not unconditional; therefore worth is not intrinsic. Conversion can be misunderstood to be a way to get God's love rather than as a celebration of having a breakthrough in understanding what it means to be intrinsically worthy. For many people, joining the church becomes a way of *having* eternal life rather than a way of relating to others who also trust in the idea of intrinsic worth. The idea of God's loving relationship with human beings gets lost in the struggle to gain that very love.

In order to prove our worthiness for God's love we have fought wars over conflicting versions of theology. At various times people were threatened, tortured, or killed for holding to alternative ways of being baptized, celebrating the Eucharist, or determining the date of Easter. People had to *have* the right membership, *know* the correct belief, and *do* the proper ritual in order for God to love them. That is the way of extrinsic worth: you must earn God's love.

This emphasis continues to undermine the idea of intrinsic worth, which holds that we don't need to *have* anything to be somebody, to be significant, to be saved. Salvation isn't a thing to *have;* salvation is *a way of being* that receives life and all of Creation as a gift, celebrates that gift, and seeks to share that understanding with all others.

The tendency to conditionalize God's love and to force the message of Jesus into a framework of extrinsic worth is much older than the American experience. But it has found a unique expression in our society where individualism and economic gain are taken to such extremes.

Econo-egocentrism reinforces pietism, which sees the only relationship to God as an individual, personal one. It ignores the concept of the "people of God" and corporate responsibility, major themes in the Hebrew scriptures, in Acts, and in Paul's reminder that we are "members one of another." Pietism refuses to take any corporate responsibility. This avoidance can be seen in the common pietistic interpretation of Matthew 25. The sheep and the goats are usually misunderstood to be images referring to individuals. But that's not what the parable says. All *nations* are called together to determine which ministered and which did not. The worldview of econo-egocentrism keeps people from taking the word "nations" seriously.

We prefer to ignore God's judgment on us as a nation, assuming instead that since "in God we trust," our policies must generally be correct. We want impunity as the "chosen people," forgetting that such a designation implies responsibility and not personal or national egocentrism. We want to have the sense of significance without having to change our understandings and actions.

Believing that we are the chosen people egocentrically separates us from the rest of the world. When we say or think that "God is on our side," we mean us as a nation, not as a world, not as humanity, not as the children of the Creator. Though it is often subconscious, we generally hold the opinion that we as a nation are favored in some way over people in other countries. Dualistic thinking enables us thus to conclude that whatever we do is right and whatever they do (if it differs from us) is wrong. These ideas not only horribly complicate and strain our foreign relations and attitude toward the rest of the world, but also muddy the theological waters of our relationship with God and with each other.

See below chapter 15, "Food for Thought," below pages 168ff., nos. 18, 56, and 62.

CHAPTER 12

Reclaiming Intrinsic Worth

There is, then, no question whether *we will have a civil religion. The only important questions are what* kind *of civil religion it will be.* —Michael Novak

If geo-communocentrism were to become our new worldview, what would serve as our bonding religion? Obviously econo-egocentrism could no longer serve this function; its values would be too antithetical to our new understanding. In a geo-communocentric society, the idea of intrinsic worth and the values of interdependence, responsibility, and cooperation would become the basis for a new bonding religion.

With such a foundation, this new religion would support a growth in the sense of community, civic virtue, and the practice of economic as well as political democracy. By stressing intrinsic worth it would support the right of each person to life, liberty, and the pursuit of happiness finally manifesting in full the vision of our founders.

The bonding religion would also be in agreement with the basic tenet of the gospel, which is that human beings are loved by God unconditionally. Such agreement would not mean that Christianity would become our bonding religion, nor that some form of Christianity would be established as a state church. To our perceptions so shaped by dualistic thinking, this seems to be the only alternative to our present situation. But this is not the case. As discussed earlier, a pluralistic society with many metaphysical religions must have a bonding religion to keep the society together. The bonding religion and the metaphysical religions must be compatible: they must share a basic understanding of life, fundamental social values and mores, and a willingness to allow the other its own sphere of influence.

Just because religions are compatible, however, it does not mean they are one and the same. Sharing an understanding of what it means to be human does not mean that the national bonding religion would give official support to specific expressions of institutional Christianity such as baptism, Lent, or Christmas. It does mean that the basic values and ideals of Christianity would be compatible with, and thus acceptable and effective in, the society.

A geo-communocentric bonding religion would stress community and hold to the idea of the intrinsic worth of all people. This would be in agreement with the gospel message and thus the basic values of intrinsic worth Christianity. It would be equally compatible with any religion that celebrates the worthiness of human beings and the sacredness of life. Thus the original ideals of most metaphysical religions in our society would find acceptance and respect (see chapter 15, no. 14).

Geo-communocentrism would offer a favorable environment for those philosophical and religious traditions that profess that God's love, or the cosmic affirmation of human beings, is unconditional. The concept of intrinsic worth, however taught in various traditions, would have a chance of being heard, understood, and lived by.

Geo-communocentrism would also offer, in the spirit of inclusiveness, a safe social environment for those institutional religions that profess that human beings must, by moral living and good works, earn God's love, or divine affirmation. Groups that teach the inherent evilness of human beings or theologies based on guilt and religious groups that thrive on a sense of superiority and exclusion would have the right to be heard. They would, of course, have to chart their course against the prevailing worldview, just as those who profess the idea of intrinsic worth do now against the values of econo-egocentrism.

Religious institutions could become the examples for the new society instead of being overwhelmed and subverted by the old. Growth in membership in the religious institutions would no longer be a priority. The quality of congregational life and the integrity and sincerity of the message and purpose of the churches would gain new importance. With synergic power as the decisional policy, everyone could contribute to the deliberations that are presently so often limited to the experts in polity and theology.

Institutional religions would not be perverted to compete with each other but could cooperate and learn from each other and respect each other's traditions and rituals. Exclusionism would tend to be replaced by ecumenism; instead of stressing the differences, the values held in common would be emphasized.

This would be important to all Americans because it would allow true freedom of religion. For those claiming no metaphysical religion, geo-communocentrism would offer a worldview of intrinsic worth and the values of responsibility and interdependence. Christians would not be influenced by the values of econo-egocentrism. The gospel message of God's unconditional love would no longer be lost in the culture dominated by the philosophy of extrinsic worth. Instead it would flower and grow in the favorable, open environment of geo-communocentrism.

What might the bonding religion look like if geo-communocentrism became our dominant worldview? Once again, there is no way to know for sure what would result, but we can project a few ideas.

The key word in the governance of the new bonding religion would be democracy — government of, by, and for the people. In a democracy there are technologists, but no technocrats. Technocrats say, "I am knowledgeable. I should make the decisions because my knowledge will make the decisions more efficient." Technologists say, "I am knowledgeable. I share my knowledge with the community to the best of my ability so that the community may decide more wisely."

As econo-egocentric governance is marked by special-interest politics, geo-communocentric governance is marked by goals determined through well-informed reflection and discussion. Included among these goals would be providing for everyone adequate nutrition, decent housing, proper health care, and an opportunity to participate in meaningful activity that is humane and creative for the individual and for the community. These essentials would not be provided because persons had proved themselves worthy of receiving them, or so that the "haves" could show off their magnanimity to the "have-nots." Essentials would be made available equitably because the recipients are of cosmic worth. They would be respected because they *are* and are therefore deserving of the basic necessities for a healthy, wholesome life.

Policy made by the public would not, of course, be foolproof. It would often suffer from communication problems, judgmental errors, and lack of information the same as policy developed by the experts. There would, however, be fewer problems caused by manipulation, hidden agendas, and power plays. In econo-egocentrism mistakes are usually handled by ignoring the accusations or by denial, as the Watergate and Iran-Contra affairs have illustrated. To confess bad policy is to lose face and self-esteem. This is why our nation "can admit of no error; it must win every argument, no matter how trivial."[1] In the new bonding religion the use of synergic power and the attitude of inclusiveness would allow us to face errors openly and creatively. This would enable us to learn from them and to address whatever problems have resulted.

Since the witness of a religion is the lifestyle through which that religion is manifested every day, the mission and witness of geo-communocentrism would be the same. How we witness to our basic values is the key to our developing any legitimate influence on the value systems of the rest of the world. Mission would take place through witness.

This understanding of mission is rooted deeply in the first tradition in images like "a City upon a Hill" and "God's New Israel." The original implication behind such images was not proselytization, but was, as John Winthrop warned in 1630, that "the eyes of all people are upon us."

We need to understand that such a mission has nothing to do with going out and changing other nations, as we have so often tried to do in the past. It has to do with our being what we need to be on behalf of our founding vision. Developing such a society is not a way of proving that we are better than others, but rather a way of pioneering for the sake of all. As Senator William Fulbright said, "If America has a service to perform in the world — and I believe she has — it is in large part the service of her own example."[2]

Our mission would be to stand before the whole world as a people who organize themselves in such a way that (1) all individuals are valued and respected because they *are,* (2) all individuals have an equal place in the political process, and (3) all individuals are sustained economically so that they may enjoy "life, liberty, and the pursuit of happiness."

Education is the process of ensuring the survival of the oncoming generation. In a geo-communocentric society education would involve training in cooperation and synergic power and the application of responsibility to everyday affairs. It would also include fostering interdependence in the relations of nations as well as the relations of family and friends and co-workers.

Instead of using inculcation to get students to have certain viewpoints, we would enable them to wrestle with diversity and conflicts in priorities. Children would be helped early in life to try new goals and learn how to evaluate their own progress. They would also learn to gain from the evaluations given them by others. Grades have no place in this process because grades are one of the inculcators of the idea of extrinsic worth.

Reading, writing, computation, and speaking skills would develop as the children needed them to make new discoveries and share their thoughts with each other. Also included as a communication skill would be listening, for what good is it to have something to say when few know how to listen?

There would be constant training in democracy as learners became involved in real issues in class, in school, and even in the community. Democracy has little meaning as an abstract academic subject. The process of responsibility becomes very real for students when the process and their decisions have actual ramifications for their lives.

As stated before, worship is that activity by which persons remind themselves of the beliefs they have about what gives life ultimate meaning. Worship, etymologically "worth-ship," is the active symbolizing of our ideas about the basis of human worth. In econo-egocentrism, the meaning of life is in becoming "somebody"; the basis of worth is what we have earned. "Worth-shipping" within the econo-egocentric framework is participating in the drive to gain the worth that will give us significance or protect the significance we feel we have acquired.

In geo-communocentrism, the meaning of life is life itself: the basis of human worth is our very existence. "Worth-shipping" in the geo-communocentric understanding is participating in any activity that celebrates life and causes us to rejoice in receiving the universe as a gift.

The various ways that people take to celebrate and express their thankfulness cannot be projected by only a few people. These ways must, if they are to be genuine, grow from all the people; in fact, the roots of the word "liturgy" mean "the work of the people." Therefore, we cannot say specifically what rituals and celebrations would be developed. We can suggest, however, that the focus of such activities would be on reverence for Creation in all its forms, thankfulness for our intrinsic worth, enjoyment of and rejoicing in the meaningfulness of life, and celebration of our human endeavors, feelings, creativity, and existence. Included in this would be celebration of specific events and persons in our national heritage. Rather than focusing only on our military and economic supremacy and the men who engineered it, we could celebrate human and social development and the persons who clearly expressed the values of interdependence, cooperation, and responsibility.

Geo-communocentric symbols would emphasize images of the awesome creativity of Creation: the night sky, the DNA double-helix, and representations in various forms of the process of human life from birth through death. We might also include symbols of our communocentric tradition and goals as a nation: the City upon a Hill, the natural beauty of the land, the Statue of Liberty in its role of welcoming the huddled masses, cooperative barn-raising, the original thirteen-star flag, the voting booth, and the view of the earth from the moon.

"Arting" would be seen as an important expression of the bonding religion. If it were entered into more as process than as product, everyone could participate without worrying about how "good" they were. With the enjoyment of the creating being more important that the result, dancing and singing, painting and miming could be the activities of all and not just a few. Other physical activity such as walking and running and swimming would also be celebrational, done for joy and health rather than as ways of determining who does what better than whom.

Envisioning what such a bonding religion might be like is difficult, but it is also exciting and inspiring. If we set out purposely and consciously to develop another worldview, we will be able, to a large extent, to determine what it will be like. It is possible to experiment with what images and rituals will make it meaningful for us.

See below chapter 15, "Food for Thought," pages 168ff., nos. 23, 26, and 47.

CHAPTER 13

Faithing Up to It

> *You may dance the tune played by the present reality. Your style of life will be realistic and pragmatic. Or you may choose to move your body under the spell of a mysterious tune and rhythm which comes from a world we do not see, the world of our hopes and aspirations.* Hope is hearing the melody of the future. Faith is to dance it.
> —Rubem Alves

As we have seen, the first step in changing our worldview is becoming aware of it, understanding why it needs to change, and realizing that such a change is possible. The second step is envisioning possibilities and potential results of the change. This step gives us a glimpse of where we might be going, which in turn offers motivation and direction to get there. At this point we may feel deeply that we need to change and we may have a powerful vision of what our society could be like. If we remain at this stage, however, the possibilities and vision will remain abstract; nothing (except, of course, our idea of what is possible) will change.

We must go one step further and make our vision a reality. This final step entails acting and making decisions based on the idea of intrinsic worth. To be able to do this we must actively trust that we really are of worth inherently and unconditionally. Being willing to trust in this alternative understanding enables us to try it out, to give it a chance, to risk seeing what might happen. Only when we let intrinsic worth affect our lives can geo-communocentrism ever become a reality.

This step of actively trusting is called "faithing." In English (and in econo-egocentrism), the word "faith" is used as a noun, a thing, something to have or to lose. It seems odd to us to use it as a verb. But in many languages the word *is* a verb, illustrating that faith is not a thing one can own but an activity that one does. In order for us to capture the sense of that activity we need to use the word as a verb in English. We can say that we "faith" in the alternative idea of intrinsic worth. To say that we faith in something means far more than believing it is true. It means that the idea affects and underlies all of our decisions, behavior, and ways of relating.

For instance, you can believe that a swinging bridge will support you and write a paper telling about your belief. You can have engineers inspect the bridge and when they declare it safe you can announce that news to the world. You can stand there for forty days and nights telling passersby that you believe the bridge to be safe. But all you will have done is to illustrate that you *believe* in the safety of the swinging bridge. It is not until you step out onto the bridge that you *"faith"* that the bridge will hold you up. *It is not the talking but the risking that is faithing.*

Faithing is more than mere believing. Faithing is believing in something to the extent that you are willing to bet your life on it.

We faith everyday. When you take a medicine that the doctor has prescribed you are faithing that the doctor was correct in the diagnosis and that the prescription was written properly. You faith that the pharmacist can decipher the doctor's writing and can fill the prescription correctly. You also faith that you can follow the directions. You are faithing because you may be risking your life that everything about the prescription is as it should be.

We faith every time we go out on the freeway. We bet our lives that all will go well when we go into the midst of eighteen-wheelers and cars whose drivers try to prove their importance by going much faster than is safe. We faith that the airplane will get us to our destination alive and in one piece. We cannot prove that someone loves us, but we faith that it is true when we trust them with our feelings and secrets, our hopes and dreams.

Though we may not have thought of it as such, we faith every day in these and many other ways. Faithing in a different world-view is the same process, only in a broader and probably more conscious form. We faith that the bridge will hold us by stepping out on it. We faith that our worth is intrinsic by ceasing the struggle to gain and protect our worth.

Whenever we faith, we have no assurance of the outcome. If we did we would not need to faith; we would know. As it is, all we have is a belief, a belief strong enough to act on. Thus, faithing is an act of courage, an act of stepping out into the unknown. Faithing in the bridge means stepping onto it *as if* it will *really* hold us up. Faithing in intrinsic worth means acting *as if* our worth is *really* intrinsic. It means acting on the belief that our lives have significance just because we are, and treating others as if they, too, are of worth intrinsically. We faith that intrinsic worth is possible by acting as though it is. This is not to say that it is not possible and that we should just pretend that it is. The point is that there is no way of knowing until we try it out.

Faithing in the vision of a geo-communocentric society means basing our relationships and attitudes on the realization that we are all interdependent. Acting responsibly and cooperatively is a way of faithing that it is possible to relate to others in these ways. We also faith in the viability of these methods when we expect others, and give them the opportunity, to respond in kind. We faith that a geo-communocentric society is possible by acting through the framework of geo-communocentrism itself. In this way we not only state that we believe it is possible. We *make it a reality.*

Some will say that it is expecting too much of people to ask them to faith in an alternative worldview that has never before been manifest fully. "Who knows what could happen? We could be heading down the path to destruction." The weakness in this argument is that by most indicators we are already headed toward destruction. *Geo-communocentrism didn't get us in this trouble, econo-egocentrism did!* We need only to point to the mess that we are in, environmentally, psychologically, and physically, to produce abundant evidence that extrinsic worth and econo-egocentrism will eventually destroy us.

Yet, in spite of the immense problems econo-egocentrism has brought us, millions faith that it is the only possible reality for the modern world. In spite of all the trouble that the search for extrinsic worth can cause, millions continue to faith that they can establish their importance by owning things, knowing things, and doing things.

If we can faith in extrinsic worth regardless of such negative results, we should be able to faith in intrinsic worth, especially considering the positive results envisioned as possible. If we can faith in that which obviously seems to be destroying us, it is hardly asking too much to try something that, though new, may offer a chance for survival.

Faithing in geo-communocentrism takes the worldview out of the abstract and causes it to be real and effective in our own small bit of society. This gives us the chance to see what might result. When we trust that our worth is intrinsic we enable ourselves to see geo-communocentrism at work.

Through our experience with this alternative perspective we may decide that geo-communocentrism is not what we want. Or we may discover that it offers possibilities that appeal to us, possibilities that we never thought viable before. Whatever we decide, we must first have the opportunity to see geo-communocentrism "in action," and this can occur only through faithing. Our acts of faithing may not bring about an entirely new social order, but they can make geo-communocentrism and intrinsic worth real in our own lives.

Things to Watch Out For

> *Our sole defense, our only weapon, is a life of integrity, whether we meet honor or dishonor, praise or blame. Called "imposters" we must be true, called "nobodies" we must be in the public eye. Never far from death, yet here we are alive, always "going through it" yet never "going under." We know sorrow, yet our joy is inextinguishable. We have "nothing to bless ourselves with," yet we bless many others with true riches. We are penniless, and yet in reality we have everything worth having.*
>
> —2 Corinthians 6:7b–10 (Phillips translation)

The process of faithing is actually a remarkably simple process, especially when considering the power and potential it has. But saying it is simple does not mean that it is easy. It is by all means possible, but it would be unfair to imply that there are no difficulties involved. There *are* difficulties, but they are not insurmountable. Being aware of potential obstacles beforehand can help us avoid them or at least minimize our frustration and discouragement.

One of the main problems in faithing, and in the worldview-changing process as a whole, is that it can be frightening. Human beings, like all animals, tend to fear that which is new and unknown, and an alternative worldview will be new territory. However much we fear them, such challenges tend to "bring out the best" in human nature. Rarely have we let trepidation keep us from attempting the new. Again and again challenges have been overcome and our society and the world have gone through many changes. One of the things we do best is adapt. So, almost in spite of ourselves, we constantly change ourselves, our society, and our environment. We are too creative, too imaginative, and too determined to survive to become totally static. More than being obstacles to change, fear and novelty may actually challenge us to try harder.

Another obstacle to faithing is that it can involve giving up the basis of our very identity. If we have always defined ourselves by success and comparison to others, how will we know who we are when we stop believing in these measurements of our worth? We must be willing to risk losing the old imprisoning definitions in order to discover the freedom of the new. We must be like the butterfly breaking open its chrysalis in order to discover its new life.

Of course, it isn't easy to change our whole way of thinking just because we want to. It is hard to think in terms of a geo-communocentric perspective because we have learned that this perspective is naive, unrealistic, and even wrong. The challenge is to overcome this bias and learn to think in another way. When learning a new language, it takes practice to think in a different vocabulary, speech patterns, and sentence structures. It also takes practice to think in terms of interdependence when egocentrism has always dominated our perceptions. It takes practice to act cooperatively when we have always been trained to compete. It takes practice and time, but we *can* become fluent in geo-communocentric thinking.

To gain such fluency we must pay close attention to words and language itself. Language is both structured by and structures the way we think. Words not only reflect but also shape our perception of reality, our worldview. Referring to the sky as "up" is a directional image shaped by pre-Columbian thinking. Yet it continues to perpetuate the illusion that we are standing on a flat plane looking "up" rather than on a ball looking "out."

Similarly, the words we use subtly create and reinforce econo-egocentric thinking. Many of us frequently use violent words and imagery such as "I could have killed him," "They really shot me down," "That blew me away," "I'd kill for a beer." Such phrases reflect the acceptance of directive power and violence in our society, but their common usage also shapes and reinforces this way of thinking, adding to the acceptability of violence simply by incorporating it into our speech. The use of the vague "they," as in "They won't let you do that," "They said it was okay," "They said it was no threat to the general populace," reflects and supports expertism. Using exclusive male pronouns to refer to everyone is a result of and strengthens the exclusionist attitude toward women.

We often use these words and phrases unthinkingly; they are, after all, just terms of speech. But subtly yet surely, the language we use begins to determine what and how we think and how we perceive the world around us. We may not consciously believe or admit that these words and images reflect our actual beliefs, but through their use we reinforce, legitimate, and become accomplices in the econo-egocentric worldview.

We can use this power of language to enhance and enact the process of changing worldviews. Careful use of words can restructure the way we think in purposeful, creative ways. "Innovative political action... consists in linguistic action, in changing the rules that link what we say to our experience."[1] Refusing to use violent words and images lightly can restructure our conceptual relations with others in peaceful, compassionate ways. Attempting to use (or invent) inclusionist pronouns (e.g., s/he) forces us to begin to think inclusively. Purposeful use of language can create new ways of thinking and perceiving the world.

Use of words and images can also enable us to face and deal more effectively with the problems facing us. Theologian Paul Tillich pointed out that naming the demons is half the struggle. If we can name what we are faced with it does not seem as frighteningly amorphous and unchallengeable. Pinpointing the difficulty through describing or naming it focuses our energies, empowers us, and is often a very crucial point in overcoming the problem. "'Racism,' for example, did not exist as a word until the 1950s and 'sexism' only entered the language in the late 1960s."[2] Naming our fears and threats not only enables discussion of them, but also empowers and encourages us to stand up to them and bring about change.

Even after we overcome our own fears and doubts about changing our worldview, we will still have to face the misunderstandings of those around us. In our egocentric society, true responsibility is viewed as impractical and cooperation is unrealistic. If you believe in interdependence you are an "idealist," a negative term for many people. Labeling is a way of digging holes to try to lower those who are different; such terms imply that what you say is to be discounted. If we faith in geo-communocentrism, these labels may be applied to us.

Our exclusionist society may tell us that we are dreamers, that we aren't able to cope with the "real world" and are trying to escape from it. With enough criticism like this we may begin to question our own motives. "Am I just trying to escape?" "Am I being silly and childish?" "Can I just not deal with reality?" What our critics don't realize is that what they call the "real world" is dysfunctional. To be able to cope with, to fit into, and to do well in a dysfunctional world is to be dysfunctional ourselves, to be blind to the seriousness of the world's problems, to be setting ourselves on the road to destruction.

Other people may not accept or understand what we are envisioning. This is to be expected. It is hard for us to give up an old paradigm and be open to and create a new one. It is just as difficult for everyone else — maybe even more so. We cannot get discouraged when even those close to us don't understand. With time they may. We can't let the lack of understanding frustrate or discourage us. It always seems easier to give up and go with the flow. But when the flow is leading over a waterfall someone has to start paddling madly upstream.

Of course, some people will not be passive about their skepticism. There will be people convinced that such questioning of the dominant worldview is heretical, subversive, or a threat to our society. Alternatives always stir up this kind of reaction in a society used to dualistic thinking. This, too, is understandable. As we can be frightened by giving up the old and trying on the new and unknown, our doing so can seem threatening to others. No one is happy to hear their reality doubted. This is especially true when the "reality" is as fervently, deeply, and religiously clung to as is econo-egocentrism. Since econo-egocentrism serves as our national religion, those who question it may be met with the same vehemence as doubters of any institutional religion. The feelings will probably flow the strongest against any denouncing of competition. Competition is the idol of our society. Anyone who questions its benefits and promise of significance will be viewed with distrust and treated with ridicule or anger.

The most subtle and therefore the most threatening obstacle we will encounter is the amazing, invisible pervasiveness of the norm of extrinsic worth and the worldview of econo-egocentrism. If we are not aware of how deeply they affect our perceptions, ideas, and lives it can be difficult to enact a real change. We may try to change our attitudes only to find that we have changed only how we express them. We could, for example, think we no longer compete while in actuality we are competing to see who can be less competitive. It may be subtle and disguised, but it is still competition. We need to be honest with ourselves, and feel secure enough to scrutinize our real motives and feelings. However, we should not expect ourselves to be perfect nor should we constantly worry about our motives. It is merely something we need to be aware of and open to.

A "superficial" change of worldviews may be worse than no change at all. People prone to such a "change" may feel bad and inadequate because they haven't been able to free themselves from the old worldview. They honestly want to be geo-communocentric, to stop competing, to escape the pressure of conformity, and to be more interdependent, but they can't seem to pull it off. They consider themselves "failures" and thus not of worth. They feel they are missing the chance to have real meaning and significance in their lives. This is the "guilt trap," the impossible attempt to lead a geo-communocentric lifestyle while still believing in extrinsic worth.

Such people think the path to worth is through responsibility, cooperation, and communocentrism and they feel guilty and inadequate when they are competitive or egocentric. They don't realize that they have missed the whole point; it just doesn't work that way. Geo-communocentrism can become our worldview after, and *only* after, we *faith* that our worth is intrinsic. The point is not that we *should* lead lives full of responsibility and cooperation. Such demands only lead to feelings of failure and guilt. The most important realization is that we are of worth just because we are; we don't have to do anything because of it. Thus there is no way to fail and no cause for guilt.

Go for It

> *"One person with a belief," said John Stuart Mill, "is equal to a force of ninety-nine who have only interests." Those "one in a hundred" people seem likely to steer us toward a very different future than most of us are as yet prepared for.* —R. E. Miles

It is inevitable that our society will change, sooner or later. Whatever the change, there will be difficulties involved. If the change occurs because we have failed to alter our path towards ecological and social disaster, the resulting difficulties may be insurmountable. If we make a conscious effort to change our society from econo-egocentrism to geo-communocentrism, we will likewise face challenges and obstacles. But, as seen above, these sorts of difficulties can be overcome. No human change, no matter how small, has ever come about without being doubted, feared, or hated to some degree. Thus the fact that there will be problems and difficulties involved should not scare, discourage, or dissuade us from faithing in intrinsic worth. We cannot hope to free ourselves from the influence of econo-egocentrism just by deciding to, or by reading a book on the matter. Changing a worldview is a very long process; for those of us raised in an econo-egocentric society we may never be completely rid of it. But this is no reason not to try.

Though dualistic thinking would suggest otherwise, it is not a matter of being either totally econo-egocentric or totally geo-communocentric. If we are exposed to both worldviews we may act under either influence, depending on the situation. As we become increasingly convinced of our intrinsic worth, our behavior and values will be more and more geo-communocentric. Changing our worldview is a step-by-step process. We cannot expect to overcome years of programming overnight; we will have to be patient. Each time we faith in our intrinsic worth, we become more convinced of its validity and more capable of faithing in it again. Each instance makes our intrinsic worth seem more real and makes faithing in it come more naturally.

Faithing is an amazingly powerful and effective process. It can change the immutable and create what never existed before. In simple acts of faithing, we can make geo-communocentrism real. If we can act on it, it exists. Faithing empowers us because it enables individuals to change their world. Each one of us cannot directly alter our society, but we can each change our personal perspective. And, because we are interdependent, any change experienced by one person affects everyone in some small way. Our acts of faithing may seem small, but they are the first, necessary steps towards a new society.

See below chapter 15, "Food for Thought," pages 168ff., nos. 10, 11, 22, 24, and 70.

CHAPTER 14

Trying It On for Size: 101 Ways of Living an Alternative Worldview

When things are seen differently, character is altered. As "mind" is renewed, "being" in its totality is affected...A metamorphosis occurs that affects the whole self. One becomes a different person with a different outlook.

— Bruce Birch and Larry Rasmussen

Faithing is a step-by-step process. We may believe that the swinging bridge is sturdy and dependable for its entire length — but we cannot trust every board at once. We faith in each step of the bridge as we get to it. Step-by-step we faith in the entire bridge, and we discover that it really will hold us up.

The same is true for faithing in an alternative worldview. As ubiquitous and complex as a worldview is, it is impossible to faith in it in its entirety or to try the whole thing out at once. We faith in it bit by bit, and by doing so we discover if the worldview really is a viable option.

Faithing in a new worldview is difficult and is not something we should expect ourselves to master easily. The dominant influence most of us have encountered in our lives is that of the idea that our worth must be earned. It is very difficult to break out of such deeply instilled patterns and ways of thinking. That's okay. We have to allow ourselves this difficulty. It is fine and acceptable to be wrapped up in and constantly influenced by the idea of extrinsic worth. It may not be much fun, but it is okay. Faithing in our intrinsic worth is not something we *ought* to do. It might enhance our life; it might offer enjoyment and freedom unknown in an extrinsic worth perspective. But it is not a moral imperative. Thinking that it is something you ought to do, or feeling guilty if you can't, will only interfere with understanding the concept of intrinsic worth.

No matter how much we may like to begin a new life of cooperation, responsibility, and interdependence immediately, we will most likely find that we continue to act out of competition, conformity, and egocentrism much of the time. This is no reason to feel guilty or to think we are failures. That's just the way life is. We are of worth just the way we are — even if that way is incorrigibly econo-egocentric. Our worth doesn't decrease even if we do not believe or cannot faith in its intrinsic, inherent nature.

As mentioned in the previous chapter, faithing involves reality and not just abstract ideas, concrete acts and decisions and not just philosophy. Thus, to faith in geo-communocentrism we must make real decisions and take real action. We feel that many books with a purpose similar to ours develop a good, abstract philosophy of how things should be different. But then too many of them leave the reader at that point, with no idea of how to make the philosophy a reality. What is needed are solid, concrete suggestions, ideas, directions, and options that can be used by the reader to experience, test, and faith the validity and viability of the philosophy.

In this final chapter we offer suggestions for where to go from here, for what to do now, for how to begin faithing in our intrinsic worth just to see what might happen. You might want to chose one a day to think about and work through. You might want to skim over all of them and pick out a few that really "speak" to you. You might want to look over the headings and concentrate on the sections that interest you the most. This chapter is for your benefit and your empowerment; use it however it best suits your needs.

The following suggestions have been organized into five sections. The first is designed to help you explore the idea of alternation. It includes examples of such experiences as well as ways of projecting how your perspective might be changed if an alternation occurred in your understanding of human worth.

The second section offers an exploration of the concepts of extrinsic and intrinsic worth, econo-egocentrism, and geo-communocentrism. These suggestions can help deepen your understanding of these concepts, their influence on our lives and society.

The third grouping will help you become aware of and sensitize you to the role econo-egocentrism and the idea of extrinsic worth play in your life. Without this sensitization, change is impossible; you must *know* what you're dealing with in order to deal with it. These questions will also help you think through the difference an experience of alternation would bring about for you personally.

The fourth section is designed to help children, or help parents and teachers help children, understand that their worth is intrinsic. Often what works for adults won't work for kids, so we've created a section specifically for them.

The fifth kind of offering is much simpler and more direct. They are suggestions of things to think about, activities to try out, leads to pursue, possibilities to explore. They are simply little ways to get started faithing in your intrinsic worth, and things to do to remind yourself of the vision of intrinsic worth and geo-communocentrism. You can come up with many more ideas and possibilities. We offer a few examples to get you started.

Alternation

The suggestions in this section can help you think through the concept and experience of alternation. They can serve as illustrations of alternation events and windows that might allow a glimpse of how life is never quite the same again after such an experience. Becoming aware of the possibility of intrinsic worth might make little difference in our outward actions, but we will never be able to totally ignore the realization that there is another way of looking at things. After seeing the new dimensions and colors offered by the idea of intrinsic worth, the actions, attitudes, and images prompted by the struggle for extrinsic worth may not seem quite so important, indisputable, or rational.

Breaching the World Taken for Granted

1. It's easy to absorb the story of Ebeneezer Scrooge at Christmas time, but try reading it or thinking about it in April or July when all the carols and decorations are not around to prompt certain feelings. Think of the experience of *alternation.* How did

Scrooge's "world taken for granted" get "breached?" What did he see that was radically different? What were the "new dimensions and colors" he experienced the "day after which life" would "never be the same again?"

Consider Scrooge's experience also in terms of intrinsic worth. How were his beliefs about his significance radically altered? Compare Scrooge's attitude before and after that fateful Christmas Eve. Look for egocentrism, competition, instrumentalism, interdependence, responsibility, and the inclusionist attitude.

2. Scrooge's experience can be interpreted as salvation. When the third spirit showed him his name on the tombstone, Scrooge was not terrified to realize that death awaited him. He was smart enough to realize that everybody dies eventually. But he suddenly saw something he hadn't realized: the irreversible tragedy and regret of a life wasted. It was at *this* point, not when he decided to change his life or when he had started to "do good," that he was "saved." Salvation is never in terms of a set of beliefs or acts but a sense of wonder and awe and freedom from the "oughts" of the past. Notice that he didn't have to do a thing to be "saved." His later actions were outer expressions of the inner transformation that had occurred. You don't have to agree with this interpretation, but keep this image in mind whenever you hear people talking about salvation.

3. Compare and contrast *A Christmas Carol* with the Jimmy Stewart movie *It's a Wonderful Life.* The stories are similar: both are Christmas tales, both involve a man who is visited by a spirit, both conclude with an alternation of sorts. But there are very important, though subtle, differences. The message in *It's a Wonderful Life* is that a person affects more people positively than he or she might realize. This is an important concept and is well expressed. However, the emphasis is on "George" coming to see that he is of value because of certain things he has done for others. He is not helped to realize that he is of value just because he is.

The message is heart-warming, especially within the confines of the extrinsic worth understanding, but it is not liberating. If after this experience George began to fail at everything he attempted, he would once again begin to doubt his value. How does this compare with the alternation experienced by Scrooge? Notice that

George was "saved" by what he had done, not by a sense of awe and wonder and freedom from the oughts of the past.

4. Two other movies that involve alternation experiences are *Mary Poppins* and *The Sound of Music.* Watch *Mary Poppins* and keep an eye out for the fundamental change that occurs for the father and the elder Mr. Dawes. Be sensitive to the contrast between the defense of extrinsic worth and the celebration of life and living. In *The Sound of Music* the sense of alternation is experienced by Baron von Trapp. What "new dimensions and colors" did he discover? Note the connection of this experience with the title of the movie. It's important to realize that new understandings often come from non-verbal experiences.

5. Movies aren't the only places to find descriptions of alternation experiences. Examine Luke 4:18–19. As in *A Christmas Carol,* these verses refer to the influence of a spirit, albeit a spirit of a different manifestation, and the outward expressions of an inner transformation. The idea of extrinsic worth could cause us to think that these missions are things we *ought* to do. What are these verses saying to us if we understand that we don't have to do anything to be significant or to be "saved"?

The Emperor's Clothes

6. Sometimes behavior that seems quite rational and reasonable from one perspective can seem non-sensical or even silly from another. Watch the news for footage of the stock exchange. What are those people doing? They are fulfilling a very important role in econo-egocentrism. They are also jumping up and down, waving their arms, yelling, and generally not having a very good time. Consider this in terms of the story of *The Emperor's New Clothes.*

Pay attention to the locker-room interviews after any televised sports event, but especially the Super Bowl and the last game of the World Series. One group of people is very happy. The other group is very sad. Why? What exactly is so great about winning? What is it that is won? What is really lost when one loses? In professional sports, monetary gain is an issue — but you can find the same intense emotions after ball games all over the country from Little

League to the NCAA "final four." How does this appear from the perspective of geo-communocentrism?

7. In the movie *Meatballs,* which takes place at a summer camp, there is a scene with Bill Murray during which he makes fun of competition and leads the chant, "It just doesn't matter." This is not only an example of an experience of alternation; it offers a good alternative to the demands of competition (even if he does use it to "get back at" the other camp). Whenever you get caught up in the desire to win or the fear of losing, just remember, "It just doesn't matter." If the competition still seems like it really matters, compare the joys of winning and the agonies of defeat with the story of the woman in Africa who had to decide which one of her twins should die so that the other could have enough food to keep living. Such a comparison is not for guilt-making but for perspective-changing.

8. Consider the shape of a gun and the explosive climax when it is used. There are many men in this country who must have a gun or they feel powerless, less than "real men." Is it unrealistic to assume that for these gun enthusiasts the weapon serves as a phallic symbol to overcome their sense of physical or psychological impotency? Could it be that missiles serve the same function on a national level? Relate this to the idea that *No one picks up a weapon — a spear, a revolver, a bomb, a word — unless he or she is afraid of something.* How do aggression, displays of strength, or military buildup appear from this perspective?

9. How often do we consider those around us in terms of "us" and "them?" We talk of management vs. labor, blacks vs. whites, communists vs. capitalists. We talk about those other applicants for the same job, the business that competes with us, the other team, *your* side of the family. Make a list of all those who are "them" to you. Think of all the ways you are different. Now think of what you have in common. Imagine you have become one of "them." What does it feel like? What would you think about "you"?

10. Walk through a department store. Make a mental list of the items that are actually useful or enhancing to life. What are the other ones for? Why do people buy them? Try the same approach in a grocery. Do we really need all those kinds of breakfast cereals? Just how many kinds of toilet tissue are necessary?

What Do You Mean?

11. Try to be aware of the subtle influence language has on our thinking. A simple choice of words can alter our entire understanding of a situation. Be sensitive to the way words shape our understanding of international affairs. What impression do you get when a government is described as a "regime" instead of an "administration"? How is the cooperative nature of a political summit distorted when media commentators wonder which leader will "blink"? When you hear such phrases, ask yourself if the impression you are getting is based more on reality or on the choice of words.

12. Listen carefully to common phrases, maxims, labels, and descriptions. What values are expressed by our choice of words: "upscale" or "expensive," "the ladder of success" or "the rat race," "the competitive edge" or "an unfair advantage," "moving up" or "keep on trucking," "it's lonely at the top" or "what goes around comes around."

13. Listen to sports reporting on TV and skim over the sports headlines in the newspaper. List the words denoting violence that are used to describe actions in what are purportedly *games:* beats, smashes, crushes, throws a bomb, wipes out, and the ever-popular "Kill the umpire!" Violent images pervade our casual speech, too. Listen carefully for statements like "I could've killed him," "I was so embarrassed I wanted to die," "Drop dead!" "We kicked some ass last night." Common use of such images makes us more comfortable with and accustomed to violent ideas, thus offering violence a degree of social acceptability. Be sensitive to situations in which you or others use such terms. Try to imagine alternative images that could convey the same emotion outside of a violent context.

14. We seem to have an addiction for "superlative-ism." Keep a list of all the superlatives you hear in the media and in conversation: the best, the worst, the longest, the shortest, the heaviest, the strongest, the greatest, the sexiest, the highest, the most expensive. Baseball statistics are wonderful examples: the most runs scored in a game with the fewest pitches, the most hits in front of the smallest crowd. Why are we so obsessed with this? (We will not offer a prize to the person with the longest list of superlatives!)

15. Compare the seven deadly sins (pride, covetousness, lust, anger, gluttony, envy, sloth) with the seven virtues (faith, hope, love, prudence, justice, temperance, fortitude). What do you think are the motivations behind each of these sins and virtues? How does our basic understanding of the source of human worth affect these actions and attitudes?

Pride is usually considered a noble and beneficial attitude in our society, and yet it is listed as one of the seven deadly sins. Maybe we need to reconsider what we mean when we use the word "pride." Look it up in a dictionary. One definition of pride is "an inordinate sense of self-importance." With such a definition, should we ever "take pride" in something? What is the difference between an inordinate sense of self-importance and a sense of cosmic significance?

16. "Playing" with scriptures is another way of seeing from a new perspective. People who are afraid of losing God's love or their worth in the eyes of others feel uncomfortable about doing this. But those who know that God's love is unconditional and their worth is intrinsic are able to see that such play is celebrational, not flippant, and that is can offer new insights and understanding.

In the first part of the Gospel of John, the word "Word" is translated from *logos*, which means "the mind of God" or the "purpose of God." In our data-oriented culture, "mind" and "purpose" are usually equated with words. But there are many other ways of expressing this same cosmic idea. Perhaps using another image might break open our understanding:

> In the beginning was the Music and the Music was with God, and the Music was God. The Music was in the beginning with God; and all things were made through the Music, and without the Music was not anything made that was made. . . . And the Music became flesh and dwelt among us. . . .

Using alternative images causes us to see from a new perspective, thereby opening up understanding and offering insights into the possibilities for receiving life with joy and thanksgiving. Try using the Dance, the Compassion, the Imagining, the Laughter, the Singing, the Celebration.

Concepts

The following suggestions can help you deepen your understanding of the major concepts discussed in this book. They include strategies for analyzing the effects of econo-egocentrism in our society, ways of being sensitive to the influence of extrinsic worth in our everyday lives, and possibilities for exploring the idea of intrinsic worth and experiencing the potential of geo-communocentrism.

Interfacing

17. Relate the various dimensions of econo-egocentrism with certain problems of our society. Look for the connections between them. Some people call this process "interfacing." For instance, what have egocentrism, competition, conformity, directive power, and instrumentalism to do with the problem of pollution? What have they to do with the problem of corruption in government? with the rampant use of alcohol and other drugs? How does the struggle for a sense of extrinsic worth underlie all of these interfacings? Not all the factors will be obvious with each problem, but each problem will connect with the search for, and the protection of, a sense of extrinsic worth.

You may wish to use a simple chart on scratch paper to help guide your thinking (see p. 142).

Egocentrism shows up very obviously in traffic behavior as drivers present a "me-first" attitude. Conformity shows up in the oft-heard opinion, "Everyone else goes over the speed limit; why shouldn't I?" Competition is evident as drivers try to be the first away from a stop light. A "me-versus-you" attitude can also be seen in expressions of directive power, the exclusionist attitude, and instrumentalism as "faster than" and "bigger than" intimidates other people on the road. There are personalized license plates that say something like: 2BAD4U. Can you see the connec-

	Traffic Behavior
Egocentrism	
Competition	
Conformity	
Dualistic thinking	
Exclusionist attitude	
Directive power	
Expertism	
Consumer ethic	
Instrumentalism	
The search for and protection of extrinsic worth	

tion of this public communication and the need to protect a fragile sense of extrinsic worth?

You can make a long list of problems to examine through such an interfacing: child abuse, homeless people, divorce, crime (including the "white-collar" sort), product testing on live animals, teenage pregnancy, the national debt. Be aware of the different ways you see these problems interfacing with the values of econo-egocentrism. Remember, our worldview pervades almost every part of our lives so keep an eye out for its influences in office politics, in church politics, in soap operas and sit coms, in attitudes toward national symbols such as the flag, in political rhetoric, in fashion, in the news, in advertising, in family dynamics, in overheard conversations, on children's playgrounds, in your own attitudes and feelings about yourself.

Examining the Old

18. Look at yourself in the back of a spoon (a silver pitcher, shiny doorknob, or Christmas tree ball will also work). Notice how your nose is so much bigger than the rest of your face. It makes you look pretty funny, doesn't it? It's even funnier if you move your face around or make different expressions. If this were the only way you could see yourself, your nose would probably begin to seem much more important than anything else on your face. Think about how egocentrism affects our perspective in a similar way.

19. Look for examples of egocentrism expressed as nationalism. This could include expressions of "We're Number 1" or America as God's chosen people. This attitude underlies the production of world maps that cut Asia in half so that North America can be in the center. It is also the cause of our ignorance of world affairs: there are more *teachers* of English in the Soviet Union than *students* of Russian in the United States. This difference cannot be accounted for by population size alone. Try naming all the Canadian provinces. Try naming two Mexican states. Try to name five African countries that are south of the Sahara. If you are like most of us, you may have trouble naming these places. If so, go look them up.

20. Be sensitive to the struggle for extrinsic worth. It is especially obvious in advertising where the "having" formula is so popular. Look for statements like "Want love? Get..." "For great looking legs, use..." Watch for more subtle forms of this message: many commercials advertising cars and trucks feature what amounts to reckless driving. What is such an ad trying to say to the potential buyer? In what ways does this message manipulate us in our search for extrinsic worth?

21. Browse through magazines such as *Brides, Seventeen, Hot Rod, GQ, Muscle and Fitness, Better Homes and Gardens.* How do the articles, ads, and even the titles try to affect the way the reader should look, act, and be? Look for subtle, *nonverbal* communications of the need for extrinsic worth: the peer acclaim for glistening dishes, the beautiful woman smiling at the man who owns the sports car, the love for and popularity of the mom who always serves a certain soft drink.

22. Watch carefully for hole-digging, especially in attempts at humor. When we were young we laughed as the coyote dug holes for the road-runner, and then fell in them himself. "Grown-up" humor often deals with digging holes as well: ethnic jokes, put-downs, practical jokes, ragging (all in fun, of course), even self-derogatory remarks. Listen for these and think about the possible causes for their popularity.

Watch reruns of *I Love Lucy, The Honeymooners, Sanford and Son, The Jeffersons,* even somewhat gentler shows such as *Family Ties* and *The Cosby Show.* Note how much of the humor is based on one character or another digging holes for others or for himself or herself. Even if the putdowns are gentle, they are still putdowns and illustrate our general discomfort in relating lovingly to others or to ourselves.

Watch reruns of *Leave It to Beaver* and watch the attitudes and actions of Eddie Haskell. It may seem funny on TV, but manipulation is a way to dig holes for others. Do you know any "Eddie Haskells"? Why do you think they act like that?

Intrinsic Worth and Geo-communocentrism

23. In looking for signs of geo-communocentrism in our present society, remember that we have *two* traditions in our heritage. It's a matter of seeing what is already a part of our life together. There is a sense of all persons being created equal, the push for civil rights for all, the deep desire for peace that needs only political leadership to bring it into the "real" world, people giving emotional support to the dying, including victims of AIDS, the retired folks known as Gray Panthers giving of themselves to make our society a better place for children, Mothers Against Drunk Driving working to engender a sense of responsibility in our attitudes toward a lethal drug.

On the individual level it's hard enough to determine what attitudes influence our own actions, much less figure out someone else's motivation. But it is interesting to look for instances of people who seem to feel that their worth is intrinsic at least some of the time. It may not be easy to tell if that is really what they are feeling. More than likely you'll just have to go on a vague sense that these people feel that life is meaningful in and of itself apart from anything they have or know or can do. They might be people in the public eye working for justice and compassion or treating others justly and compassionately. Or they might be people you know personally who seem to feel very comfortable with themselves and are thus comfortable to be around. In all probability they will work out of an intrinsic worth perspective only part of the time, but that's only to be expected. Keep a mental record of these individuals and how they act. Being aware of such examples can be inspiring and enjoyable.

24. Read Galatians 5:19–23. This reading seems to work out of a body/spirit dualism, but it does offer insights into how our understanding or our worth underlies our acts, attitudes, and ways of relating. How could the "fruit of the spirit" also be the fruit of understanding our cosmic significance? How could the "works of the flesh" (Galatians 5:19–21) be manifestations of econo-egocentric values? How are they motivated by the struggle for extrinsic worth?

25. Be alert for manifestations of geo-communocentric values. You might see someone stopping to help a stranded motorist, or a co-worker talking through a conflict with you, or black and white children playing together, or a successful recycling project. Look for these things and remember them — maybe even write them down. Then whenever you begin to despair about our society, look at this list.

26. Brainstorm all the jobs you can think of that *you* feel offer "real" work. By our definition, real work is that which is meaningful to us and which we enjoy, which eases suffering, and/or enhances life, and is not done simply for the money or the prestige. Everyone's interpretation of what could be real work will be different because what is meaningful or pleasurable for one person may not be for another.

Do you feel that you are involved in real work? Most of us are blocked from doing what is meaningful to us because of economic considerations. To enable the free exploration and expression involved in real work, we might have to develop a national guaranteed income policy. From an econo-egocentric perspective this idea seems ludicrous. What do you think would happen to our society if we adopted such a program immediately? From the viewpoint of geo-communocentrism, this policy begins to seem much more sensible and feasible. What would you do if *you* had a guaranteed annual income? Do you think most people would behave as you would if they faithed in their intrinsic worth?

27. Jot down all the ways you can think of that you are interdependent with others, globally as well as locally.

28. Choose a problem facing your local or global community. How many answers to the problem have you heard suggested by the experts? Brainstorm as many possible solutions as you can imagine. Don't worry if they seem impractical; even the most offbeat can sometimes open up new ways of thinking or at least offer useful images. A high school student, assigned to write a four-page paper on how to end world hunger, thought of writing one word on each page: "Feed... All... People... Equally!" It didn't solve the problem of world hunger (nor did it solve the problem of what to turn in for the assignment), but it does offer a message that is powerful in its simplicity and, obviously, one that could work if it were implemented. See how many solutions you can come up with to the problem you select.

29. Celebrating is an important facet of the intrinsic worth understanding. Look for the different ways you see people celebrating. How and what do you celebrate? Be sensitive to the fact that "partying" and "celebrating" are not necessarily the same thing. They differ in attitude and motivation if not in outward appearance.

Celebrating the good times (Christmas, weddings, Friday night) seems to come naturally. But what about the rest of our lives? How can we celebrate the bad, dull, painful, confusing, or just everyday times? All times are part of life, part of the blessing of Creation, and therefore worth celebrating. Celebrating can mean saying "Amen" to the experience. This does not mean resigning yourself to the situation, but accepting it as part of life and getting through it as creatively and humanely as possible.

Celebration can also mean savoring. Even dull, mundane times can be celebrated by savoring the blessing that is Creation in its daily manifestations. Savor an orange. It's not just part of your lunch; it is a gift full of juice and wonder. Eat it as a celebration. Celebrate by savoring life around you: stretching, a drink of water, a cool breeze, lying down at night, the ability to see or hear or move, the sunrise or sunset, your dog running up to greet you. Try savoring one thing each day. Remember, life itself is reason for celebration.

Our Personal Worldview

After familiarizing and sensitizing ourselves to the philosophy and effects of extrinsic worth and deepening our understanding of the potential of the intrinsic worth worldview, we can begin to explore the influence the idea of extrinsic worth has on our own lives.

This is not easy to do. Some of the ways we try to gain worth are obvious to us. Others are more subtle, more deeply ingrained in our sense of identity, more vital to our sense of worth. It is hard to be aware of such influences and even harder to think of changing them. This is understandable and is to be expected. However, if we want to experience the possibility of faithing in our intrinsic worth, we must first be aware of and admit how we are influenced by the idea of extrinsic worth.

There is no need to feel guilty or inadequate if we find our lives are greatly affected and directed by this search for worth. Remember that it's okay to be influenced by our dominant worldview. We are socialized to think in the ways of the worldview; its values surround us constantly.

The purpose of looking at how our worldview affects us personally is not to make us feel bad, but to make us aware. No problem can be dealt with until it is recognized. This section is designed to enable realization of the effect of extrinsic worth in our lives and exploration of a few small ways we can begin to free ourselves to faith in our intrinsic worth.

The Care and Feeding of Your Extrinsic Worth

30. The idea of extrinsic worth constantly tells us that our only significance comes from what we have or can do. What do you have that makes you feel important (material possessions, experiences, relationships, positions)? What can you do or have you done that makes you feel of worth?

Make a list of what you have or can do that you feel makes your life significant. Try to be honest, but don't be brutal. Examining our sense of worth has to be a step-by-step process, peeling off one layer at a time. Write down the ones you can think of. The list you make may be incomplete, but it can offer a suggestion of how the idea of extrinsic worth pervades and affects your life.

31. Are any of the factors that you feel give you significance things that can be lost (a good job, the school record for the 100-yard-dash, a great figure, a girlfriend or boyfriend, stock market investments)? Do you fear that someday you might lose them? Does this fear affect what you do each day? Your long-term goals? Does it affect your enjoyment of the activity, possession, or relationship itself?

32. Imagine what it would be like if, for just one day, you did not have to worry about keeping your worth secure. Would you relate to your friends more honestly if you weren't afraid of losing them? Would you feel you could be more creative with your job if you weren't afraid of risking your position? Would you be able to really enjoy a hot fudge sundae if it weren't flavored by the fear of dreaded calories? How would these changes alter your feelings of security and enjoyment of life? Would you do things differently?

33. The belief that we must constantly search for our worth tends to instill feelings of inadequacy. Do you feel you are "not good enough" in some way (looks, abilities, achievements)? Are there things you would like to change about yourself? Why? You might feel that you don't like the way you are; you might feel that others will like you better if you change; you might just have a vague sense that you should be different in order to please someone somehow for some reason.

Make a list of what you would like to have or be able to do that you feel would enhance your worth (getting a date for New Year's Eve, losing weight before swimsuit season, passing a test, getting a promotion, winning a particular case, writing a book).

34. Choose one small way that you feel inadequate. For an hour (or maybe a day) try to pretend it just doesn't matter. Did it make any difference in how you spent your time, what you thought about, your attitude toward yourself, your sense of worth? If one of your friends felt "not good enough" in this way, would you agree with her, or would you encourage her not to worry about it? Don't be so hard on yourself.

35. Reflecting on the lists you have made, think about all the things that you do to try to enhance your significance. Do you spend a lot of time and energy trying to overcome your perceived shortcomings? It's easy to feel that this is what you *should* do, but is it really what you *want* to do?

Think about what you value most in life. Then think about where you spend most of your time. Do you spend a majority of your time involved with what matters most to you? Or do you end up spending lots of time doing things that, in the long run, really aren't that important? If this is true, ask yourself why you do these things. How would you spend your time if you could do those things you value the most?

36. Make a list of your time commitments: family, job, church, committees, friends. Is there anything that you are involved in *only* because you feel it "makes you look good," "will look good on your resumé," or "is the expected thing to do"? Ask yourself if you really think it's worth it.

37. Make another list — this time of all the things that you would love to do but just don't have the time. It might be learning to play guitar, going to the park, getting rid of all that accumulated junk in the basement, reading a book, taking a pottery class, learning about the moons of Jupiter, visiting your great-aunt. Are these things important enough to you not to let them just pass you by while you are involved in other, less attractive though seemingly more pressing pursuits? Choose one or two and see if you can squeeze them in. One half hour a week doesn't sound like much, but it adds up to over twenty-four hours in the course of a year. Remind yourself that celebrating and expressing who you are is *not* a waste of time.

38. Consider all those things that you might do if your significance would not be threatened. Choose one of them, a "smaller" one, one that takes less money, time, and risk. It could be dancing in the park even though everyone will probably think you are strange. It could be wearing the same outfit twice in one week. It could be saying, "I love you" to someone. Try it and see what happens. Maybe you could try one a week. Wednesday is usually pretty boring; you could make it your off-beat day.

Accepting Your Cosmic Significance

39. Many of us find it hard to think of positive things about ourselves. We have no trouble listing our faults and failings. But when it comes to our talents and enjoyments, things we like about ourselves and ways we are special, we tend either to feel awkward talking about them or else we can't even think of any.

Pretend that you feel that your worth really is intrinsic. Suppose that no matter what you lack your worth and significance will always be the same. Now list your positive attributes. To make it even harder, try to avoid anything extrinsic. Focus on things you *like* about yourself, not things you are *proud* of. Post this list on your bathroom mirror.

40. Let yourself feel good about yourself. You have an entire worldview telling you that you should not think like this, but it's okay. Try it. See how it feels. When you start to get blocked by your "faults" remember they cannot detract from your worth at all — and go look at the list on your bathroom mirror.

41. Sidney Simon says that many people cannot offer validating statements to themselves or to others because they are so used to using putdowns or "killer" statements. Putting down oneself is what he calls "vulturing." It is one way people keep themselves in holes thinking, "If I'm already in a hole maybe I can't fall any farther." Putting down others he calls "vipering." To the person who faiths in intrinsic worth such statements will seem strange and counter-productive. Do you find yourself vulturing or vipering? You may think they are strange and counter-productive and still find yourself using these put-downs. That's understandable; it is acceptable and expected behavior in our econo-egocentric society. Think about ways you can validate yourself and others instead.

42. Think back to your school days. What was elementary school like? What feelings do you remember most? For most of us junior high was a rough go, and high school only a bit better. Most people have mixed memories of being in school; many have overwhelmingly negative ones. Why is this? A time of learning and discovery could be very exciting and enjoyable — but often it is not.

Jot down some of the feelings or events that you remember from school. Do you recall anyone telling you that your worth was intrinsic? Do you remember feeling required, by teachers or classmates, to prove your significance in some way? Were you encouraged to compete or to cooperate? Did you feel included or excluded? Did you feel that you were being expected to do things or be a certain way? Do you remember falling in any holes? Falling in holes was probably the most common experience in school; kids are frighteningly good at making each other feel inferior or uncomfortable.

Think through these memories. Some may be painful, but could things have gone differently if you, your classmates, and your teachers had felt intrinsically significant? For most kids, things haven't changed much. Remembering how it was in school may also help you understand your children or grandchildren better.

43. "Try it on for size...." Pretend for awhile that you are *convinced* that your worth is intrinsic,...that you are important because you *are*,...that you are significant because you are the result of the universe working for 15 billion years to create you. It might take some practice to be able to imagine what it would be like to think this way, but it is the only way to see through the new perspective and feel your sense of belonging in the universe.

Go forth into Creation and think to a tree, "You and I are co-creatures, made from the same star-stuff!" Think to a bug, "You and I are cousins!" Look at the night sky and say to yourself, "I am a part of all this! All of this and I are one! All of this and I are eternally significant!" (If you can't go outside for some reason, look out the window, think with pictures, use your imagination, or say these things to a pet, a houseplant, a fellow human being.)

Bridging the Holes and Filling the Gaps

44. In how many instances does the perceived need to gain and protect your worth affect the quality of your relationships with family, friends, romantic interests? Think through some of the problems you may have in these relationships. How can you see these relationships being affected by egocentrism? instrumentalism? conformity? directive power?

45. How often have you found yourself trapped in a pitched battle with your parents, spouse, children to see who could "win," to see who could control the situation? Why did this occur? How did you happen to get pulled into the competition? Imagine yourself in one of these situations. What would happen if you, the other person, or both of you together faithed in your intrinsic worth and felt no need to try to win? Would it ease the tension between you?

46. Problems that we face in our relationships are not just caused by *our* search for extrinsic worth. We run into problems because others are influenced by the intrinsic worth perspective as well. Because they, like us, are out to win their worth as best they can, we find ourselves falling into holes that have been dug for us.

Try to think of the different ways other people have dug holes for us: putdowns and insults, making us lose, not respecting our humanness, not giving us a chance, saying "I told you so." How did it make you feel? How did you respond?

47. With the intrinsic worth understanding there are no such things as holes. If "falling in a hole" is the process of feeling we're losing worth, then those who believe they can never lose worth will not easily fall into one. Keep in mind that, given the way we were trained, you will most likely fall into many more holes in your lifetime. Even faithing in intrinsic worth does not obliterate years of thought and behavior patterns based on extrinsic worth. Please remember that emotionally falling into a hole while intellectually clutching the concept of intrinsic worth is a very natural thing to do and should be expected.

With this in mind, remember a particular instance in which you fell in a hole. Now try to picture what would have happened had you felt your worth could not be lost. Could you have told yourself that the hole really wasn't there? Would you have felt as threatened by the situation? What difference would it have made if you had faithed in your intrinsic worth and refused to let the hole exist for you? How could you possibly experiment with this process for future "hole" situations?

For Kids

Children are just as influenced by econo-egocentrism as are adults. They are bombarded by advertising, they are encouraged to compete, they are overwhelmed by expertism and directive power, and they sense what the adults around them feel is important. Children are involved in the process of absorbing experiences and information, imprinting what it means to live in our society. Because of this, they may be more sensitive than adults to the influences of econo-egocentrism. For this same reason, they are more readily open to learning new ways of relating, new understandings, new values.

Some of the following suggestions are things that older children can do on their own. Most of them are suggestions of how parents, teachers, and others can avoid reinforcing extrinsic worth values and can help children feel their own intrinsic worth, be alert for the influence of the extrinsic worth idea, and experience and explore life through the geo-communocentric values. (Number 6, 18, 41, 71, 80, 86, 90, and 99 might also be useful for children and parents.)

What Does Intrinsic Worth Feel Like?

48. The best way for children to gain the understanding that their worth is intrinsic is to grow up around adults who faith in their own intrinsic worth. Kids pick up on our attitudes and values more than most of us suspect. They will pattern their behavior and beliefs more on how you act than on what you say.

It is very important for all of us to feel that we are significant, but it is crucial for children. Children are developing a sense of identity, they have little experience to fall back on in times of doubt, and they feel even more vulnerable than adults in a big, strange world. Most younger children have little need of hearing that their cosmic worth is intrinsic or that God's love is unconditional. They need to know that their parents', grandparents', guardians' love is unconditional. If your child feels accepted and loved by you as she is, she will feel cosmically accepted as well. With such a base of self-esteem, she will be more able to understand her intrinsic worth and God's unconditional love when these concepts become an issue for her.

49. The terms "intrinsic worth" and "unconditional love" won't make sense to most kids. Think of ways to translate these ideas into an eight-year-old's language: I will always love you even when you do something that makes me sad or angry. God loves you forever and ever, no matter what. You are important wherever you are, whatever you do, whatever you think. Unconditional love is someone inviting you to his birthday party even if you won't let him play with your toys.

50. Ask your child to tell you what he likes about himself. Maybe you can write what he says on a big piece of paper, or if your child can't read, you and he can draw pictures to symbolize each attribute. If any that he lists are things that can be lost, let him know that you like these things, too, but that you will love him even if he no longer has or does them. If he likes the idea, you and he can hang the paper on his bedroom wall.

51. Familiarize yourself with the main concepts of Transactional Analysis. There's *TA for Tots* and *TA for Kids* as well as various *TA* books for adults. Help your children to understand and identify the difference between "doing strokes" and "being strokes." The images of "warm fuzzies" and "cold pricklies" can help children express their feelings. Being able to express their feelings, and have them listened to and valued, enables children to feel significant and important.

52. Contrast the stories of Winnie the Pooh and the Ugly Duckling. In the Winnie the Pooh stories, none of the animals are ever banished from the forest, excluded, required to change, or in any way made to feel unaccepted. Eeyore excludes himself and is grumpy about it, but everyone loves him anyway and respects his right to be as he is. Some of the animals had trouble dealing with Tigger when he first came to the forest, but in the end they all grew to love him. This happened not because of anything he had done to prove his acceptability (he had gotten Roo stuck up in a tree and had bounced Rabbit into the river), but just because of his Tiggerness.

How do these stories compare with the one about the Ugly Duckling? The "duckling" is excluded and made to feel inferior because he looks different. It is only when he grows up and proves that he is actually a swan (swans presumably being higher than ducks in the waterfowl hierarchy) that he is accepted, and it is the ducks who feel less important. Unfortunately, most children may have felt they were treated more like the Ugly Duckling than like Tigger when playing with other children. But which values, which attitudes toward oneself and others, do you want to reinforce in your child?

53. Older children, becoming aware that we are tiny creatures on a planet that is a mere speck circling a small star off on the edge of the galaxy, may be amazed (or even bothered) by how insignificant we seem compared to the immensity of the universe. Encourage them to look at it another way: Compared to the atoms in our thumbs, we ourselves are immense. We are the result of the original Creation fireburst the same as all other parts of the universe. From the atoms in our thumbs to the farthest galaxy, all parts are of utmost value and importance! How big we are and where we are and what we are doing makes no difference in significance.

54. Christmas should be a time of celebrating the good news that our worth is intrinsic. Jesus was not born in extrinsically significant surroundings. This blessing did not occur because humanity had earned it. However, to most children — including Christian children — the important idea during this holiday is not that God gave us an amazing gift because God loves us, but that Santa will give many gifts because we have been good. Listen to the words of *Santa Claus Is Coming to Town.* Does this song reinforce a child's sense of cosmic significance or the need to prove and earn something?

At Christmastime try to focus on a child's inherent goodness. Using the reward of Santa's gifts to modify behavior invites feelings of insecurity and reinforces the idea of extrinsic worth. Christmas will be much more celebrational for your child if Santa's gifts are unconditional. Remember, the original St. Nicholas gave without regard to "goodness," but according to need.

Expose your child to the intrinsic worth message of Christmas as much as possible. The Christmas story itself is a good source of this idea — especially if it hasn't been "adapted" to talk about how the donkey earned the right to carry Mary.

Collect other Christmas stories that have this underlying message. The story *Why the Chimes Rang* illustrates this idea even though it has its extrinsic worth interpretations. The chimes rang for the gift of the child not because the gift was particularly noble in its lowly form but because it was the only gift whose giver was not competing for the prestige of making the bells ring. Watch or read *How the Grinch Stole Christmas* and watch for the experience of alternation. Notice how the Grinch was saved not by anything he had done, but in spite of everything he had done. Watch out for the story of *Rudolph,* however. Rudolph is excluded and considered insignificant until he proves that he can do something important. Help your child, and yourself, guard against the extrinsic worth perversion of Christmas. Celebrate the blessing of intrinsic worth.

Growing Up Geo-communocentric

55. Make a "having" formula collage. If you sit down on the floor with some paper and scissors and glue and start leafing through a big stack of old magazines, it probably won't be long before your kids will want to help. Tell them you are looking for advertisements that seem to promise things that aren't true. Or tell them you are looking for ads that seem to promise magic: If you buy this kind of car you will magically get a beautiful girlfriend. If you smoke this cigarette you will magically become a cowboy. Once they become sensitized to this message they won't easily forget it.

56. Keep in mind that your children will pick up your values more from what you do than from what you encourage them to do. Saying, "Do it because I say so" reinforces and trains your child to accept expertism. Spanking is hitting, and hitting is a form of directive power. Children will learn from this that it is okay to hit in order to control other people. Remember, values are caught, not taught.

57. If competition causes problems in your family or class (someone is upset because she lost a game or wasn't first in line), point it out to the kids. Talk about the problems with competing: only one person can be first, only one person can win; that means everyone else is sad. Help them think through other possibilities where more people can be happy.

Try not to reinforce competition by using it to motivate children. Capturing the fancy of their natural imagination and curiosity is less manipulative and works much better anyway. Instead of saying, "Let's see who can get to the car first," try saying, "Let's all walk like spiders to the car."

58. Kick around a soccer ball without trying to score. See how many balls you and your friends can keep going at once. Try cross-country soccer, or relay soccer, or blind-folded soccer. Set up two or even three or four goals and see how many points you and your friends can make within ten minutes. Create different strategies that will enable as many scores as possible. Focus on the fun of playing, the celebration of physical activity, the appreciation of skill and cooperation, and the fact that no one has to lose.

59. Schools put more emphasis on grades than on learning, assuming that the grades will reveal how much has been learned. This results in children not being interested in the excitement of learning, but in the establishing certain levels of worth, indicated by the grades they receive. How often have you heard one child ask another, "Whadja get?" Adding to this uncertainty of who is better than whom is a fact we all know from experience: an "A" with one teacher may be a "B−" with another. What is needed is a complete rejection of grades and the extrinsic worth burden that they carry. Instead, we need to help children learn the *process* of setting reasonable goals for their learning and to help them think through how they will recognize when they have reached those goals. This is a synergic power activity and, if our children are to experience it, it may have to take place at home.

Sit down with your kids and ask them what they are interested in, what they would like to learn about it. They might be interested in dinosaurs, fishing, pirates, space, where Grandma lives, how to make cookies. Help them think through all the different ways they could explore these interests. They might want to get books out of the library, look through an atlas, watch a TV show on the subject, draw pictures, read stories, put on a play, pretend to be a certain character for a day, or have you teach them to make cookies. Help them get started but let them go at their own pace, following their own imagination and curiosity. Keep checking with them on how its going — your enthusiasm and support will encourage them and help them feel that what they are doing is interesting and worthwhile — but don't overdo it, especially with older kids.

Chat with your children about the goals they set, whether they feel they reached them, and if not, why not. Help them see that errors and mistakes are learning tools and that being afraid to be wrong kills creativity. Help them realize that all this learning took place without grades!

60. Children often think that there is only one right way to do something. This may be because they get "corrected" so frequently. Try not to label a child's actions or ideas as "wrong" unless they are directly harmful to herself or others. Be aware of your own dualistic thinking; try to appreciate and understand what the child has done as a creative alternative and an example of her imagination and intelligence.

Play games of divergent thinking: list ten fruits and see how many ways you can group them (color, taste, shape, where they come from, where they grow on the plant); brainstorm as many uses as you can for a flowerpot (hold open a door, a hat, holder for a small flagpole), how many different kinds of transport can get you from one place to another (riding different kinds of animals, flying carpet, crawling, hopping on a pogo stick), how many different routes could you follow?

61. Note how many "horror films" are showing at any one time in your movie theaters or on TV. These films reinforce the traditional dualistic thinking about good and evil. A lot of these movies are made to cater to older children and young teens. Using the ideas about Creation as blessing and the intrinsic dignity of all the parts of the universe, what symbols, rituals, and celebrations might be possible to counter the influence of these films?

For younger children, there are the traditional folk tales, which have roots deep in the Indo-European emphasis on a constant struggle between Good and Evil. Princesses, dragons, sorcerers, goblins, and knights are replaced today on TV in violent confrontations between evil forces set out to rule the universe and the caped humans and friendly robots who fight against them in a never-ending struggle. Since we will see around us whatever we believe is in our worldview, children need to believe that the universe is good as it has been created.

Evil actions come from people not being able to trust their inherent significance and therefore are not able to believe that others are inherently worthy of respect and compassion. Discuss with them the fact that in real life there isn't always a "good guy" and a "bad guy." Usually, both "sides" have some truth and some falsehood.

62. Include kids in the making of as many family or classroom decisions as possible. The best way to learn democracy is to participate in it. Feeling respected enough to be included will encourage responsibility and reinforce feelings of worth.

63. Kids are often inundated and overwhelmed by econo-egocentrism every day at school. Helping them think through what is going on can help them deal creatively with the situations they face. Reinforcing your belief in their intrinsic worth can help counter-balance the extrinsic worth messages they receive all day long. Help your children become aware of directive power both on the playground and in the classroom. Encourage them to ask questions. Explain to them that being excluded from a group comes not from their faults, but from the group's need to feel "better than" somebody. Support their ability to play cooperatively. Help them to understand that selling candles or candy is not their duty to the school, class, or organization but is a subtle way of training them to conform to the economy. And above all, make sure your kids know that your love and acceptance of them is not influenced one iota by the grades they make. Such geo-communocentric reinforcement can enable your children to "be in, but not of, this world" in a very creative, affirming, confident way.

64. Read *Farewell to Shady Glade* and *The Wump World* by Bill Peet. Kids are generally sensitive to the plight of animals and will understand the problems of what happens when people want more and more.

65. Pick up trash along a path or stream. Make it unto a treasure hunt; there's no reason why something useful can't also be fun. Point out how much better the area looks after you've finished. Most kids will enjoy this activity and will gain in a sense of responsibility, interdependence, and the reverence ethic.

66. Find biographies or stories about men and women who have saved endangered species, worked for justice, created parks, made medical discoveries, stood up for what they believed. Expose your child to non-military, non-sports heroes like Harriet Tubman, John Muir, Susan B. Anthony, Francis of Assisi, Bartolomé de las Casas, Roger Williams, and Jacques Costeau.

67. Encourage children's talents and foster their creative expression. Avoid comparing or critiquing their artwork. Appreciate it as an expression of who they are.

68. A stuffed cloth planet made of polyester and cotton and printed in bright non-toxic colors is available for purchase. Young children will enjoy it and become geo-conscious at the same time. You can find the planet through peace groups or through speciality toy stores.

Faithing

Because the concept of extrinsic worth is so strong in our culture, faithing in the concept of intrinsic worth means we must continually sharpen our understanding of econo-egocentrism. We must also continually reinforce our growing ability to think and act within the framework of geo-communocentrism. This section offers possibilities for you to further clarify your understanding and apply this understanding to everyday life.

Some of these suggestions involve thinking, others involve doing. Some may "speak" to you, others may not. Find the ones that help you remain sensitized to the omnipresence of econo-egocentrism. Find the ones that illuminate the idea of intrinsic worth for your life. Find those that empower and encourage you day to day. Have fun.

69. We "faith" each time we go out on a highway. We literally bet our lives that we will be safe. Compile a list of the various ways you "faith" each day.

70. Think inclusively. Find a city or other place in each of the twenty-four times zones around the world. (A time zone is theoretically 15 degrees of longitude.) Discover something about what it is like to live there. Find out some of the political, economic, cultural, geographic, and historical factors that block or enhance a humane future for the people who live there.

71. Try to say "geo-communocentrism" five times — fast.

72. Read Matthew 6:21. Keeping this in mind consider the fact that the people of the United States make up 6 percent of the world's population, yet we use 30 percent of the world's resources expended each year. In what ways is this fact connected to our econo-egocentric worldview? How would our daily life be affected if we cut our consumption of these resources by half, down to 15 percent? This would still be more than double our fair share. Could we get by with half the fuel, half the electricity, half the food, half the clothing? What changes are needed in public policy that might move us to the 15 percent level? Try out a few small ways by which you think you can reduce your consumption of resources: recycle cans, newspaper, glass; walk when you can; turn out lights you aren't using.

73. Write letters to your great grandchildren or to the grandchildren of friends, or to anyone who will be living in 2040 or 2080. Tell them how the world is now and what you are doing to ensure they will inherit a humane world. Set up a plan by which these letters will get to designated recipients: keep them with your will, mention them in your will, put them in a safe deposit box.

74. Take a walk every day, or once or twice a week, and watch the changes of the seasons and how they affect the sky, the plants and trees, the animals, and your fellow humans.

75. Write your senators and representatives. Maybe you do not have anything to say, but you can check to see if *they* do. Remember, our founders believed that democracy is government of, by, and for informed people, and you are one of the people. It's your responsibility to be informed.

76. Watch the changes in the weather, both out your window and on TV. We are all equal when it comes to storms, temperature, droughts. Remember, the rain falls on both the just and the unjust, on both the Soviets and the Americans. Call TV stations and newspapers that show only the United States on weather maps and ask why. Ask them where they think the weather was before it got to us.

77. Practice devoting at least one full minute to people in your life as you greet them after they have been away from you. This comes naturally when they have been away for a long time. It's easy to forget when they have just returned from work or school or play. Devote time to them also when they are about to leave you. (See *Contact* by Leonard Zunin.)

78. Find some things that can serve to remind you that you are intrinsically worthy. You may wish to choose items in your home or place of work. You may wish to design a symbol that can be your reminder. Or you can use something of nature like thinking of the breeze as a bringer of change, the warmth of the sun as inspiration for growing and celebrating, or the night sky as the confirmer of your sense of oneness with all.

79. Recycle your trash and garbage. Most cities have several places that will pay for your aluminum cans, newspapers, and glass. If you do not have a recycling center near you, consider starting one. You needn't buy all the equipment. Just designate a collection point in town or in the community and contact the closest recycling center. They will probably come pick it up.

Your garbage can be mulched. Plastic butter dishes make great sand toys; donate them to a day care center. Re-use envelopes; it is possible to turn them inside out, but it's a lot easier to tape over or scratch through the old address.

80. Recast the rules of games in order to turn them from competitive to cooperative efforts. A game should be fun and not frustrating. When faced with different playing abilities, play in terms of the inclusionist attitude, synergic power, and the reverence ethic.

- *Yahtzee:* play for the highest combined score; take turns filling in one game; discuss the pros and cons of where to place a score. Beware of placing blame on someone for an unsuccessful roll of the dice.
- *Othello:* strategize to come as close as possible to an even score: 32–32.
- *Double Solitaire:* cooperate by sharing cards so that both persons have a better chance of finding cards that they need.
- *Monopoly:* let the bank own all the utilities, railroads, and the most and the least expensive properties with hotels; no one plays the banker; players seek to help each other stay afloat by cooperating and pooling resources; players are successful if all are still in the game after reaching a predetermined time limit.
- *Scrabble:* let the highest combined score be the goal; share ideas and swap letters.
- *Pool:* cooperate in sinking all the balls in some agreed order; each player can be restricted to one side or to one side and one end; discuss who has the best shot at the next ball to be played; you can play against the clock to see how long it takes to sink all the balls.
- *Boggle:* play as usual except the scoring should be a total of all players; the reading of the lists of words should be from the shortest list to the longest; in this way even those who are not as adept can add to the total.
- *Ping Pong:* see how long the players can keep the ball going from person to person (this idea can be adapted for tennis and badminton); if the ball gets off the table "cross-country ping pong" can be played until the players can get it back to the table (this is probably best played outside).

81. Spend more time with your pet. Speak to friendly pets in the neighborhood. Name a plant. Having a non-human friend is a great way to expand your inclusionist attitude and your sense of the oneness of all things.

82. Find a picture of yourself when you were two or three. Is that person in the picture of worth? significant? important? If that little person were someone else asking for your love would you give it? Can you give your love to that little person inside you? Remember, that's you! You are the same person with the same basic feelings.

83. Choose a country you know nothing about. Read about it in an encyclopedia. Look for it in the news. Become that country's ambassador to your family and friends.

84. Go swimming and don't swim laps. If you are an adult, try remembering how you played in the water when you were a kid. Have fun! If you're a kid, teach an adult how to play.

85. Take a moment to think about something you usually take for granted, like gravity, or the wind, or the way your body takes sound waves and turns them into music or birds singing or traffic noises. We usually don't even notice, but Creation is incredibly amazing.

86. Lie on your back and look at the night sky. Watch the stars. Imagine yourself attached to the side of a huge ball looking not *up* but straight *out.* Try this some night when there is going to be a meteor shower. Unfortunately for those of us who like to sleep a lot, the best time for viewing meteors is after midnight.

87. Read some *Winnie the Pooh* stories. Read them out loud to others. Serve milk and cookies.

88. Think of your talents. Dust off one that you haven't celebrated in a while: try out the musical instrument you haven't played since high school, draw with crayons, toss a baseball around, compose a song, give someone a back rub, make someone feel special.

89. Look through your photo album with pictures of yourself when you were younger. Think of yourself as an exciting, developing, significant person. Don't lament your mistakes; making mistakes is a part of life and learning. Remember, you've never lived this life before; you never got a chance to practice. Follow your journey through your life to the present moment. Do you realize that you are browsing through the biography of a unique, significant, irreplaceable, and very human member of the world community?

90. When worms get washed up on the driveway or sidewalk during a big rain, pick them up and put them back in the grass. Icky or not, they are our cousins and sometimes need our help. It's nice to feel you can help alleviate suffering in some small way.

91. Make sure your home has maps on the wall. These are not just for your own use, but for the enlightenment of others who may not realize that people cannot be geo-communocentric without having some sense of the "geo" on which we live. In a day when so many people cannot find where they live on a map this service of posting maps is very important. Hang a map of your city or neighborhood; juxtapose it with a map of the same area fifty or a hundred years ago (if you can find one.)

See what the astronauts see. Get a world map with no political divisions showing. Savor the beauty of this earth as a whole entity. Think about the fact that governmental boundaries are concepts and do not exist. They have no meaning to deer and trees and fish and thunderstorms, only to humans who put up fences thinking they have created something amazing when all they have created is fences. Familiarize yourself with where you live in terms of geological and ecological areas instead of political ones. Get a star map. Familiarize yourself with your astro-neighborhood.

92. For at least one meal a week, try to eat slowly. Savor your food. Take time to enjoy the flavors, the aromas, the textures. Celebrating eating is a way of living through the reverence ethic. If we eat as most do, we are relating to food instrumentally; we are being mere consumers (i.e., "devourers"). If you prepare meals, take time to savor the experience, again noting the flavors, aromas, and textures. Cooking with a reverential attitude will make a big difference in the way you relate to all other beings on this earth.

93. People can be excluded as much by what is not said as by what is said. Many women feel negated by the use of masculine pronouns supposedly to signify everyone. There are definite linguistic and grammatical problems involved in changing this practice, but try using feminine pronouns in such instances just for a day. See if it offers a new perspective.

94. The Native American of the plains would sing a song to the buffalo he had just killed, thanking it for its gift of life so that his family might have food and warmth in winter. We rarely kill our own meat these days, so it becomes very unusual for any of us to think reverentially about the food we eat. To sing a song to the cow while standing in the supermarket or in a fastfood place would strike us, and others, as strange. Nevertheless, even in such an antiseptic atmosphere we are still life feeding on life and we would do well to recognize this. How can you thank the cow or the chicken for the nourishment you receive? What rituals could you create that would enable you to reverence the life that gives you life?

95. Loan your copy of this book to a colleague, a friend, or a family member and encourage them to read it. When you're trying to change your society, or at least your small part of it, it's helpful to have someone who supports and understands you. Another way to find support for your envisioning or companionship for your faithing is to contact a group involved in geocommunocentric activity. Several notable examples on the national and international scale are Amnesty International, Food First, the Fellowship of Reconciliation, Global Education Associates, and Friends of Creation Spirituality. (The addresses of these groups can be found at the end of this book.) There are probably numerous organizations in your community that stress cooperation and interdependence and that are interested in restructuring our society to be more humane. Look them up. They might need you, and you might appreciate the support and the companionship.

96. Write a poem... *not* to please a teacher or some other "authority," but just to play with words and ideas. Remember that fear is the biggest enemy of creativity!

97. Follow an ant. Ants have intrinsic worth too, as a part of Creation. Do you think this ant realizes it?

98. Do things that don't accomplish anything in terms of the work ethic. Blow bubbles, play with a slinky, listen to a bird singing, watch a sunset.

99. Try not to smush harmless spiders. If you find one inside, and you prefer not to have it around, trap it in a plastic cup, gently slip a piece of thin cardboard under the cup, and take it outside.

100. Without checking your makeup, or straightening your tie, or looking to see if your hair is the way you want it, smile at yourself in the mirror.

101. Three or four times a day say to yourself: "I am significant, important, of worth. Nothing can change that. No matter what happens, I am of worth!"

CHAPTER 15

Food for Thought: 70 Brief Insights for Personal Reflection or Group Discussion

Food for thought for breakfast. It sure beats cream of wheat.
—David Leftkowitz

This chapter offers a variety of quotations for the purpose of augmenting and supplementing the presentation of the concepts in the other chapters. It is hoped that they will enhance your understanding of this argument and the need for changing our worldview from econo-egocentrism to geo-communocentrism.

We have not put these quotes in any order; we thought that variety and contrast would make them more interesting. If you are looking for quotes that pertain to specific concepts, you can refer to the numbers at the end of each chapter. Otherwise you might want to take each one of these quotations in order or you can browse around till you find one that strikes you as being particularly interesting. You may find some that are of no interest to you at all. That's okay. Maybe some of the quotations scattered through the other chapters will be helpful.

What you do with a quotation is up to you, but we suggest that it be considered in terms of concepts such as econo-egocentrism, or the reverence ethic, or Creation as blessing. You may find you can relate some of these thoughts to what you discover in experimenting with the suggestions in chapter 14. You may wish to set a certain time period each day or each week for consideration of the ones that speak to you. A group meeting to discuss this book may find that sharing personal selections from this chapter may be helpful. Or, at each meeting of the group, certain quotes can be chosen to discuss in relation to the book's concepts.

We offer these quotes simply as food for thought. We think you will find them interesting and pleasurable. We hope that you also find some of them thought-provoking, illuminating, and inspiring. Enjoy.

1. We can say without exaggeration that the present national ambition of the United States is unemployment. People live for quitting time, for weekends, for vacations, and for retirement; moreover, this ambition seems to be classless, as true in executive suites as on the assembly lines. One works, not because the work is necessary, valuable, useful to a desirable end, or because one loves to do it, but only to be able to quit — a condition that a saner time would regard as infernal, a condemnation. This is explained, of course, by the dullness of the work, by the loss of responsibility for, or credit for, or knowledge of the thing made. What can be the status of the working small farmer in a nation whose motto is a sigh of relief: "Thank God it's Friday?"

— Wendell Berry, *Home Economics,* p. 166

2. Jesus' love for the poor and the oppressed was not an exclusive love; it was an indication of the fact that what he valued was humanity, not status and prestige. The poor and oppressed had nothing to recommend them except their humanity and sufferings. Jesus was also concerned about the middle and upper classes — not because they were especially important people but because they too were people. He wanted them to strip themselves of their false values, of their wealth and prestige, in order to become real people. Jesus wished to replace the "worldly" value of prestige by the "godly" value of people as people.

— Albert Nolan, *Jesus Before Christianity,* p. 57

3. Our institutions are designed to turn out experts and other brilliant mediocrities whose distinguishing characteristic is what Thorstein Veblen called "trained incapacity" to see beyond their professional blinders.

— William Ophuls, *Ecology and the Politics of Scarcity,* p. 243

4. When classes, races, ideologies, nations, or other corporate entities clash, little civility is shown. Dealing with this type of conflict is both the most urgent and the most baffling problem of the contemporary world. To date, education has been of little help. For the most part it has been dominated by nationalistic, ideological, religious, or class consciousness. Narrow loyalties rather than civility have shaped the curricula of the world. We have American, Russian, Chinese education, but few schools in which allegiance to the human good is viewed as the prime value to be learned.

—Sam Keen, *To a Dancing God,* p. 65

5. A mind divided by choices, confused by alternatives, is a mind robbed of power. The body reflects this. The ambiguous person is a machine out of phase, working against itself and tearing itself up. That person is an engine with sand in its crankcase, broken piston rods, water in its fuel lines. In spite of great effort and noise, nothing much happens.

—Joseph Chilton Pearce, *The Crack in the Cosmic Egg,* p. 13

6. Advertising...is an institutionalized and highly creative effort to create greed in a person and in society. And greed will always lead to competition in oneself, that is, a gnawing dissatisfaction with what one already possesses, and therefore its very starting point is one of *creating dissatisfaction.* Advertisers do not want to win us over to loving something we already are or already have, but they begin by convincing us that we are not yet what we should be because we do not yet have what we ought to have.

—Matthew Fox, *A Spirituality Named Compassion,* p. 208

7. The central fact about the middle classes is this: that they are not, in fact, middle class at all. They are middle-income workers, and while their physical lot is far, far better than that of their brothers and sisters in other parts of the world, they are still tied to the predominant economic machine with a short leash. When it coughs, they jump. When it no longer wants to produce what they are trained to manufacture, they adapt or sink. When it begins to ail, they feel the pain.

—Adam Finnerty, *No More Plastic Jesus,* p. 74.

8. The good worker does not share the industrial contempt for "raw material." The good worker loves the board before it becomes a table, loves the tree before it yields the board, loves the forest before it gives up the tree.

—Wendell Berry, *Home Economics,* p. 144

9. What...artists, visionaries, and saints are all involved in is the resacralization of culture. The sacred reconnects the part to the whole, the part to the universe. The profane is that which has become loose, fallen off, or been broken off from the whole. With those pieces people try to build up a thing called "reality," but it's always a hodge-podge of fragments. Science, Marxism, or any zealous ideological movement, tries to connect fragment to fragment and then tries to hold it together with spit or sweat or other people's blood, but it always comes apart sooner or later. The more mystical way is to realize that you can't force it. The fish with a memory of the ocean cannot reconnect his puddle to the sea. He can only speak of oceans and wait for the tide—and that's quite a different role from the unbending revolutionary who is going to put everything together in an egotistical solution.

—William Irwin Thompson, *The Celtic Consciousness* (Robert O'Driscoll), p. 602

10. The need for balance "is symptomatic of a basic distrust that anything good can come out of disorder. In a sense, this represents a distrust of creation, for in creation order does issue from chaos. Without the new connections that are made possible by the disruption of old patterns, nothing can be born."

—Lois Robbins, *Waking Up in the Age of Creativity,* p. 74

11. Grandma said when you come on something that is good, first thing to do is share it with whoever you can find; that way, the good spreads out to where no telling it will go. Which is right.

—Forrest Carter, *The Education of Little Tree,* p. 57

12. The American dream is often a very private dream of being the star, the uniquely successful and admirable one, the one who stands out from the crowd of ordinary folk who don't know how. And since we have believed in that dream for a long time and worked very hard to make it come true, it is hard for us to give it up, even though it contradicts another dream that we have — that of living in a society that would really be worth living in.

— Robert Bellah et al., *Habits of the Heart,* p. 285

13. "Occupational accountability" means we will not allow our labor to go into making products which kill others.... We will take a close look at what we are producing to determine if it is safe and ecologically sound. We should also consider our choice of a career, and whether it contributes concretely to a better world for all humankind. If our present occupation does not do so or is only marginally helpful to others, we may decide to change it even if we earn less money as a result.

— Adam Finnerty, *No More Plastic Jesus,* p. 201

14. The first World Conference on Religion and Peace in Kyoto, Japan, in 1970 brought together almost five hundred leaders from the world religions — Buddhism, Christianity, Hinduism, Islam, Jainism, Judaism, Shintoism, Sikhism, and Zoroastrianism... Using their religious and ethical insights, the delegates adopted the Kyoto Message... which outlines the common ground that exists for... world religions to join hands in the task of building a human world order:

> As we sat down together facing the overriding issues of peace we discovered that the things which unite us are more important than the things which divide us. We found that we share:
>
> - A conviction of the fundamental unity of the human family, and the equality and dignity of all human beings;
> - A sense of the sacredness of the individual person and his conscience;
> - A sense of the value of the human community;
> - A realization that might is not right; that human power is not self-sufficient and absolute;
> - A belief that love, compassion, selflessness, and the force of inner truthfulness and of the spirit have ul-

timately greater power than hate, enmity, and self-interest;

- A sense of obligation to stand on the side of the poor and the oppressed as against the rich and the oppressors; and

- A profound hope that good will will finally prevail.

— Gerald and Patricia Mische,
Toward a Human World Order, pp. 315–316

15. The ultimate significance, meaning, security, value, dignity of my life is not dependent upon anything I can do, make or accomplish. Therefore, my action may spring out of what I am rather than arising out of a desperate need to establish myself.

— Sam Keen, *To a Dancing God,* p. 131

16. One person up can awaken another
Who can then awaken a sister or brother.
The three of them can raise such a fuss
They finally awaken the rest of us.
The rest of us can raise the town
By turning the whole place upside down.
One person up with stars in the eyes —
Multiplies!

— from *For Heaven's Sake* (adapted)

17. Preach faith *till* you have it; and then *because* you have it, you *will* preach faith.

— Peter Buehler, *The Journal of John Wesley*
(Nehemiah Carnock), p. 442

18. Look at the reverse of the Great Seal of the United States, which is on the dollar bill. You see an unfinished pyramid, representing the American national enterprise, and over it the all-seeing eye of God. Most impressive are the mottoes, in Latin naturally: "Annuit Coeptis," "He (God) has smiled upon our beginnings"; and "Novus Ordo Seclorum," "A New Order of the Ages." That is America in America's civil religion: a new order initiated under God, and flourishing under his benevolent providence. Could the national and the religious be more combined; is it at all possible to separate the religious and the national in this civil religion, any more than it was in ancient Greece and Rome?

—Will Herberg, *American Civil Religion* (Richey and Jones), p. 80

19. As we lie in bed each morning, we awake to the fire that created all the stars. Our principal moral act is to cherish this fire, the source of our transformation, our selves, our society, our species, and our planet.... This is the central fire of yourself, the central fire of the entire cosmos: it must not be wasted on trivialities or revenge, resentment, or despair. We have the power to *forge* cosmic fire. What can compare with such a destiny?

—Brian Swimme, *The Universe Is a Green Dragon,* pp. 169–170

20. For women to pump up their biceps or break into the club of hard-driving money grubbers on Wall Street is a peculiar and sad kind of liberation. For the feminine voice to slide down into a baritone that rasps about being number one is a poor excuse for deliverance. The fact that women's values have tended to clash with the demands of competitive, male-dominated institutions does not mean that the former ought to adjust to fit the latter.... I trust that women will choose to stop learning competition, that in its place they will truly affirm relationship. This time around, maybe the lesson will be cooperation and men will be the students.

—Alfie Kohn, *No Contest,* pp. 180–181

21. Only a psychology of celebration yields compassionate persons because it is in celebration that we learn to forget our self-consciousness, our bodies, our egos, our fears, our problems, our self-images, our positions of status or lack of status — and remember our ultimate wholeness and therefore holiness. For all celebration is an act of forgetting in order to remember.

—Matthew Fox, *A Spirituality Named Compassion,* p. 89

22. Faith is nothing else but a right understanding of our being—trusting and allowing things to be; a right understanding that we are in God and God, whom we do not see, is in us.

—Julian of Norwich, *Meditations with Julian of Norwich* (Brendan Doyle), p. 89

23. The authentic religious impulse is neither self-righteous nor passive. It is actively truth-seeking in both a deeply personal sense and in its mode of participation in the human community.... To be truth-seeking is to be empty and open. It is to trust that persons are called to love, unity, justice, truth... and that these can be realized if we do not allow self-centered attachments to obstruct the way. To be truth-seeking is to be able to assess our most cherished assumptions and move beyond idolatrous attachment to nationalism and ideology.

—Gerald and Patricia Mische, *Toward a Human World Order,* pp. 343–344

24. If the alternative version of reality exists only in the minds of a few individuals, it can be dismissed as fantasy, and the persons who expound it can be told to "get back in touch with reality." However, if a reasonably large number of people begin to act and interact on the basis of an alternative version of reality, their actions could make the official reality transparent. Institutions, after all, do not exist independently of the human beings who externalize themselves by creating social worlds. When human beings begin to interact on the basis of different perceptions of reality, institutions change or disappear.

—Kevin D. Kelly, *Youth, Humanism and Technology,* pp. 21–22

25. We become rich precisely to the degree that we eliminate violence, greed, and pride from our lives. When we have rediscovered this primordial wealth we shall see something the wise have always known: the earth is, always has been, and always will be more beautiful than it is useful.

—William Ophuls, *Ecology and the Politics of Scarcity,* p. 244

26. What is the alternative to an economics of competition? A letting be, a letting go, a celebrating. An interdependence based on mutual sharing of the pleasures of the good earth instead of their mutual hoarding.

—Matthew Fox, *A Spirituality Named Compassion,* p. 89

27. To fraternize with all creatures as Francis did means, to use the apt expression of Paul Ricoeur: "seeking to transform all hostility into a brotherly tension, within the unity of God's creation." . . . It means to opt definitively for a world where unity must in the end win out over division and dislocation; it means refusing to hoist oneself above others and to treat them like things, in a universe where "the mystery of the earth touches that of the stars."

— Eloi Leclerc, *Francis of Assisi: Return to the Gospel,* p. 133

28. "Self-belittlers'" . . . internalized Parents constantly remind them that they should "behave," mind their manners, be content with what they deserve. Whenever they receive anything they don't deserve — when they get ahead temporarily, or even win — they are made to feel guilty and therefore depressed. They soon learn that to avoid further pain and feelings of alienation they must keep their place.

— Stuart Walker, *Winning: The Psychology of Competition,* p. 250

29. Anxiety might be seen as a psychiatric symptom, but it might also be seen as an appropriate response to an insane world. We may need more revolutionaries and fewer psychotherapists.

— Philip Norman, *The Earlhamite,* Summer 1987, p. 19

30. I remember Yvonne Dilling, a U.S. church worker who spent two years with Salvadoran refugees in Honduras, telling me about the structure in the refugee camps. As soon as the refugees began to make a new camp, they set up three committees. There was the committee of education and the committee of construction. And there was the *Comité de Alegría,* the "committee of joy." Celebration was as basic to the life of the refugees as teaching their children to read or building a latrine

One refugee woman once asked Yvonne why she was so serious all the time, why she walked around looking so burdened down. Yvonne talked — as I am sure any of us would have — about the tremendous suffering of the people, the grief that she felt every day, and her commitment to give all of herself to the struggle of the refugees. And this woman looked at her and just said, "You're not serious about our struggle. Only people who expect to go back to North America in a year work the way you do. You cannot be serious about the struggle unless you play and celebrate and do those things that make it possible to give a lifetime to it."

—Joyce Hollyday, *Sojourners* magazine, June 1987, p. 34

31. Basic training does not begin in boot camp. It begins in kindergarten. It continues with a vengeance for the subsequent twelve years. —Jonathan Kozol, *The Night Is Dark and I Am far from Home,* p. 61

32. "Those who humble themselves will be exalted" is not a promise of future prestige to those who have no prestige now or to those who have given up all reliance upon prestige. It is the promise that they will no longer be treated as inferior but will receive full recognition as human beings. Just as the poor are not promised wealth but the full satisfaction of their needs—no one shall be in want; so the little ones are not promised status and prestige but the full recognition of their dignity as human beings. To achieve this a total and radical re-structuring of society would be required.

—Albert Nolan, *Jesus Before Christianity,* pp. 57–58

33. [Sin can consist of] the refusal to love oneself well, the refusal to celebrate both one's dignity and responsibility. When people sin in this way they become suckers for hero worship, for projecting onto others their own dignity as images of God. Whether these others are matinee idols or religious ones, whether alive or dead, makes no difference. The sin of refusal to acknowledge one's own dignity remains the same. Without healthy self-love there will be no other love. —Matthew Fox, *Original Blessing,* p. 120

34. Women...are buying into the competitive system rather than challenging it. "Buying into" is an apt phrase, in fact: The case of woman and competition is not merely analogous to, but part of, the question of privilege. Pseudofeminism may celebrate competition in women's athletics or competition in the abstract, but it is primarily concerned with competition for money. The current call to become competitive cannot be differentiated from the acceptance (and thus the perpetuation) of our economic system. Pseudofeminism is, in its consequence if not in its intention, a conservative movement. —Alfie Kohn, *No Contest,* p. 180.

35. The Amish community . . . is based on the love of neighbors, of creatures, and of places. The community accomplishes the productive work that is necessary to any economy; the economy supports and preserves the land and the people. The economy cannot prey on the community; it *is* the community. . . . The economic helpfulness, the charity, that is natural to the life of a community — and free to members — . . . has been replaced, among most of the rest of us, by the insurance industry.

— Wendell Berry, *Home Economics,* p. 189

36. A life composed mainly of work that lacks much intrinsic meaning and leisure devoted to golf and bridge does have limitations. It is hard to find in it the kind of story or narrative, as of pilgrimage or quest, that many cultures have used to link private and public; present, past, and future; and the life of the individual to the life of society and the meaning of the cosmos.

— Robert Bellah et al., *Habits of the Heart,* p. 83

37. Sportsmanship is an artificial concept. It would not exist except for competition. Only within the framework of trying to win is it meaningful to talk about carrying this out in a graceful or virtuous fashion. If we did not compete, we would not have to try to curb the effects of competition by invoking sportsmanship; we might well be working *with* other people in the first place.

— Alfie Kohn, *No Contest,* p. 164

38. Jesus . . . was the hero of love, a hero without power, who did not use force, who did not want to rule, who did not want to *have* anything. He was a hero of being, of giving, or sharing.

— Erich Fromm, *To Have or to Be?,* p. 141

39. Members of the underclass in America often seem less interested in ending a system of privilege than in becoming privileged themselves. They rarely challenge the basic script, preferring to concentrate only on the casting. The economic system that predicates wealth on poverty, power on powerlessness, is implicitly accepted even by those with the greatest incentive to challenge it. This is a tribute to the effectiveness of our society's ideological apparatus, which encourages debate on tiny questions in order to deflect attention from the big ones, and which . . . perpetuates a myth of individual responsibility to the exclusion of attention on structural causes. — Alfie Kohn, *No Contest,* p. 180

40. Robert Fox, priest, street theologian and bard, has said that pornography is just the tip of the iceberg that makes visible the profound connections between violence and the loss of intimate sexuality. "If we choose not to touch tenderly, then we will touch violently because we must touch, and be touched, to survive. If we are not about caring, we will be about competition. If we are not about tenderness, we will be about violence."

— Marcia Lovelace Tolva, *Creation,*
July/August 1985, p. 17

41. To be true to work and the depth of its task we need always to make clear that the greatest thing to come out of the factory is the factory worker; the greatest thing to emerge from the mine is the miner; the greatest thing to come out of the farm is the farmer. To miss this essential value is to confuse means with ends and to make idols of our work.

— Matthew Fox and Brian Swimme, *Manifesto for a Global Civilization,* p. 48

42. The revolutionary function of education is in continual danger of being submerged because it is always the generation with vested interests in the old that is in charge of educating the young.... In a democratic society the older generation conserves its values most effectively by forming a conspiracy of silence, by prohibiting the crucial questions from arising. The repressive, the reactionary function of the educational system is not so much what is done in schools as what is not done. The vacuum rather than the whip is the instrument of preserving the status quo. The whip, sooner or later, creates a rebellion which has the effect of binding the rebel to the value alternatives which are conceivable within the system against which he is rebelling. The true revolution could only be created by asking the central question of the meaning of human existence from a perspective which is alien to both the establishment and those who are locked in rebellion against the establishment. Freedom lies beyond conformity or rebellion.

— Sam Keen, *To a Dancing God,* p. 41

43. If, in searching for self-fulfillment the citizens of a "free country" like America pay attention only to the private self, they are not free. —Daniel Yankelovich, *New Rules,* p. 222

44. Day care centers are cheaper than prisons. That's what it comes down to. It costs $35,000 a year to keep someone behind bars. Wouldn't it have been more sensible to spend a few thousand dollars a year for the first seven years of that person's life? We'd have developed a taxpayer, not a criminal.

—Bob Keeshan, *Nashville Tennessean,* Feb. 23, 1988

45. When we take the whole universe as our frame of reference, we begin to appreciate the cosmic significance of running water. Only by establishing ourselves within the unfolding cosmos as a whole can we begin to discover the meaning and significance of ordinary things.

—Brian Swimme, *The Universe Is a Green Dragon,* p. 31

46. Comparisons are the enemy of creativity.

—Lois Robbins, *Waking Up in the Age of Creativity,* p. 82

47. The kingdom of God... will be a society in which there will be no prestige and no status, no division of people into inferior and superior. Everyone will be loved and respected, not because of his education or wealth or ancestry or authority or rank or virtue or other achievements, but because he like everybody else is a person.... Those who could not bear to have beggars, former prostitutes, servants, women and children treated as their equals, who could not live without feeling superior to at least some people, would simply not be at home in God's kingdom as Jesus understood it. —Albert Nolan, *Jesus Before Christianity,* p. 58

48. A bright young lawyer (or a bright old lawyer, for that matter) whose work consists in helping one corporation outwit another is intelligent enough to doubt the social utility of what he or she is doing. The work may be interesting — even challenging and exciting — yet its intrinsic meaninglessness in any larger moral or social context necessarily produces an alienation that is only partly assuaged by the relatively large income of corporate lawyers.

— Robert Bellah et al., *Habits of the Heart,* p. 288

49. Jesus provides a dream that includes and explains failure. It says the bottom line is people come together under God's care rather than as individuals making it under their own self-propulsion. — John C. Haughey, *Wall Street Journal,* June 29, 1987

50. The Indian never fishes or hunts for sport, only for food. Grandpa said it was the silliest damn thing in the world to go around killing something for sport. He said the whole thing, more than likely, was thought up by politicians between wars when they wasn't gittin people killed so they could keep their hand in on the killing. Grandpa said that idjits taken it up without a lick of thinking at it, but if you could check it out — politicians started it. Which is likely.

— Forrest Carter, *The Education of Little Tree,* p. 107

51. Our lives are not merely affected by, but structured upon, the need to be "better than." We seem to have reached a point where doing our jobs, educating our children, and even relaxing on the weekends have to take place in the context of a struggle where some must lose. That there might be other ways to do these things is hard for us to imagine — or rather it *would* be hard if we were sufficiently reflective about our competitiveness to think about alternatives in the first place. Mostly we just accept it as the way life is. — Alfie Kohn, *No Contest,* p. 3

52. Human beings are not on earth to manufacture consumer items for one another but to share being; to celebrate being; to reverence being; and to fall ever more deeply in love and thankfulness for being. — Matthew Fox and Brian Swimme, *Manifesto for a Global Civilization,* p. 49

53. A Declaration of Interdependence: "When in the course of human events it becomes necessary for one people to move beyond their national self-consciousness and relate to all the peoples and powers on earth of equal station to which the laws of Nature and

Nature's God have called them, a decent respect of the opinions of humankind requires that they should declare the causes which impel them toward oneness.

"We hold these truths to be self-evident, that all persons are created equal, that they are endowed by their Creator with certain inalienable rights, that among these are life, liberty, equal opportunity, self-development and the pursuit of meaning. That to secure these rights, Governments have been instituted among persons, deriving their just powers from the consent of the governed, that whenever structures of government, social and economic systems or concepts of national honor and loyalty become destructive to these ends, it is the right of the People to alter or abolish them, and to institute a new Government, laying its foundation on such principles and organizing its powers in such forms, as to them shall seem most likely to effect global justice and the well being of persons everywhere."

—James Armstrong, *The Nation Yet to Be,* p. 100

54. Growth is the secular religion of American society, providing a social goal, a basis for political solidarity, and a source of individual motivation; the pursuit of happiness has come to be defined almost exclusively in material terms, and the entire society—individuals, enterprises, the government itself—has an enormous vested interest in the continuation of growth.

—William Ophuls, *Ecology and the Politics of Scarcity,* p. 185

55. Classic republican theory from Aristotle to the American founders rested on the assumption that free institutions could survive in a society only if there were a rough equality of condition, that extremes of wealth and poverty are incompatible with a republic.

—Robert Bellah et al., *Habits of the Heart,* p. 285

56. The mystics rose above the repressive idea of God's judgement and demand of justification from humanity; they understood that God does not need the justification of human beings but the love of human beings and the transfiguration of their nature. This is the central problem of Christian consciousness. Is the essence of Christianity in justification, in judgement, in God's implacable justice? Or is this essence in real transfiguration and illumination in God's unending love?

—Nicolas Berdyaev, *Western Spirituality* (Matthew Fox), p. 128

57. God showed me in my palm a little thing round as a ball about the size of a hazelnut. I looked at it with the eye of my understanding and asked myself: "What is this thing?" And I was answered: "It is everything that is created." I wondered how it could survive since it seemed so little it could suddenly disintegrate into nothing. The answer came: "It endures and ever will endure, because God loves it." And so everything has being because of God's love. —Julian of Norwich, *Meditations with Julian of Norwich* (Brendan Doyle), p. 25

58. The world is not a realm of powers who are our adversaries. All creation participates in the goodness that God as creator intended for the world. —Bruce Birch and Larry Rasmussen, *The Predicament of the Prosperous,* p. 113

59. Blessing is politically dangerous; the art of savoring is politically suspect; pleasure is too often a route to sharing the pleasure — which is justice-making. And justice-making conjures up passionate criticism of what is. As W. H. Auden put it, "As a rule it was the pleasure-haters who became unjust." The prophets and others who disturbed the status quo did not only seek justice. They sought blessing, blessing for the many, not just for the few.

—Matthew Fox, *Original Blessing,* pp. 54–55

60. Through the ages, mystics of every shade of religious belief have spoken of unity, of an underlying connectedness between things: between men and women, between us and the other creatures and even inanimate matter as well, a fitting together according to an ordinarily invisible fabric underlying the cosmos.

—Scott Peck, *New Age Journal*, June 1987, p. 50

61. There can be no doubt that Jesus was a remarkably cheerful person and that his joy, like his faith and hope, was infectious.... The poor and the oppressed and anyone else who was not too hung up on "respectability" found the company of Jesus a liberating experience of sheer joy.... He made them feel safe and secure. It was not necessary to fear evil spirits, evil men or storms on the lake. They did not have to worry about how they would be clothed or what they would eat or about falling sick. It is remarkable how frequently Jesus is said to have reassured and encouraged them with words like: "Don't be afraid," "Don't worry" or "Cheer up." ... Jesus not only healed them and forgave them, he also dispelled their fears and relieved them of their worries. His very presence had liberated them.

—Albert Nolan, *Jesus Before Christianity,* p. 42

62. It is one thing to trust in God because one depends on Him in reality, and quite another to assume that He will bless our bombs because the Russians are atheists and He cannot possibly approve of atheism.

—Thomas Merton, *Conjectures of a Guilty Bystander,* p. 253

63. But if our hearts shall turn away so that we will not obey, but shall be seduced and worship... other Gods, our pleasures, and profits, and serve them; it is propounded unto us this day, we shall surely perish out of the good Land whither we pass over this vast Sea to possess it. —John Winthrop, 1630

64. To steal Elton Trueblood's term, this state religion is not an independent growth but is a "cut-flower" religion. The flowers that have been grown in the Christian Church, the Jewish synagogue, and the groves of the great humanist philosophers are cropped and used to grace the temple of the state religion — the passion for justice, the dignity of the human person, the hatred of tyranny, the demand for freedom, the love of neighbor, the tolerance of difference, the pursuit of world peace, compassion for the needy. These are not the products of any state religion of the last two hundred years but are rooted in faiths that go back three thousand years and more. Divorced from their native origins, detached from their theological roots, they are likely to wither and die.

—James D. Smart, *The Cultural Subversion of the Biblical Faith,* p. 101

65. One way of looking at sin is as a refusal to grow. It is a refusal to take on the activities and tasks of Becoming more fully.

It is to make an absolute, a false god, of the present form and way of being, thereby blocking God's creative process in and through us.... It is the historic tragedy of human potential unrealized.

—Gerald and Patricia Mische, *Toward a Human World Order,* p. 346

66. Justice pertains to both human/human and human/nonhuman worlds in a single network of relationships.... Still, we hardly know how to think about justice as a category pertaining to the nonhuman world, even though our day-to-day actions do in fact tie the destiny of human and nonhuman together. Our anthropocentric perception needs to shift to biocentric perception, justice for the full community of life.

—Bruce Birch and Larry Rasmussen, *The Predicament of the Prosperous,* p. 182

67. To those who followed Columbus and Cortez, the New World truly seemed incredible, not only because of what civilization had made of the Old World but because of the natural endowments of the one they now began to enter. The land often announced itself with a heavy scent miles out into the ocean, and the coasting whites with their nostrils full of salt and the sour odors of confinement recorded their delight with the odors of forests and verges in bloom. Giovanni di Verrazano in 1524 smelled the cedars of the East Coast a hundred leagues out. Raleigh's colonists scented what they thought a garden, though they would soon enough make it something else. The men of Henry Hudson's *Half Moon* were temporarily disarmed by the fragrance of the New Jersey shore, while ships running farther up the coast occasionally swam through large beds of floating flowers.

Had they been other than they were, they might have written a new mythology here. As it was, they took inventory....

—Frederick Turner, *Beyond Geography,* p. 256

68. Some people laughed to see the alteration in him, but he let them laugh, and little heeded them, for he was wise enough to know that nothing ever happened on this globe, for good, at which some people did not have their fill of laughter in the outset; and knowing that such as these would be blind anyway, he thought it quite as well that they should wrinkle up their eyes in grins, as have the malady in less attractive forms. His own heart laughed, and that was quite enough for him.

—Charles Dickens, *A Christmas Carol,* p. 128

69. The Creator God is a gracious, an abundant, and a generous host/hostess. She has spread out for our delight a banquet that was twenty billion years in the making. A banquet of rivers and lakes, of rain and sunshine, of rich earth and of amazing flowers, of handsome trees and of dancing fishes, of contemplative animals and whistling winds, of dry and wet seasons, or cold and hot climates.... It works for our benefit if we behave toward it as reverent guests. God has declared that this banquet is "very good" and so are we, blessings ourselves, invited to the banquet.

—Matthew Fox, *Original Blessing,* pp. 112–113

70. In an important sense, we have little recourse. Our choices *will reverberate* on into the lives of the children unto the third and fourth generations. *Whatever* our basic perception is, the effects will be registered in future lives. That makes our present choices, our dreaming and acting, critically important over a wide expanse of space and time. The responsibility, whether accepted or ignored, is awesome.

—Bruce Birch and Larry Rasmussen, *The Predicament of the Prosperous,* pp. 73–74.

Readings, Listenings, and Contacts

Readings

Wendell Berry, *Home Economics* (San Francisco: North Point Press, 1987). A collection of essays exploring the idea of interdependence from the perspective of a poet and Kentucky farmer. To Berry, the world is made up of households; thus any process of destruction or healing must begin at home.

Bruce Birch and Larry Rasmussen, *The Predicament of the Prosperous* (Philadelphia: Westminster Press, 1978). The authors express the need for a change in lifestyle based on a radical change in basic values.

Forrest Carter, *The Education of Little Tree* (Albuquerque: University of New Mexico Press, 1986). An autobiographical account of a small boy's life with his Cherokee grandparents in the Tennessee mountains. A beautiful mystical account of relationship with, and reverence for, the land and all its creatures.

Matthew Fox, *Original Blessing* (Santa Fe: Bear & Co., 1983). A complete exploration of the tradition of Creation-centered spirituality as a humane and healing alternative to fall-redemption theology.

Erich Fromm, *To Have or to Be?* (New York: Harper & Row, 1976). A provocative examination of the two ways of valuing people — their having or their being. Fromm explores the alternatives from both psychological and religious perspectives.

Thomas Gordon, *Parent Effectiveness Training* (New York: New American Library, 1975). This book can help you understand the concepts of respect and dignity in all relationships, not just with children. The sections on "how to talk so kids will listen to you," "active listening," "who owns the problem?", and "I-messages" may contribute to a sense of alternation. Good for practicing democracy.

Elizabeth Dodson Gray, *Green Paradise Lost* (Wellesley, Mass.: Roundtable Press, 1979). Takes a feminist look at how our images and words can keep us locked in the old or can free us for a new understanding of our lives and the cosmos.

Alfie Kohn, *No Contest* (Boston: Houghton Mifflin, 1986). A condemnation of competition as destructive, learned behavior. Kohn explores how competition pervades our society, causing innumerable personal and social problems.

William Ophuls, *Ecology and the Politics of Scarcity* (San Francisco: W. H. Freeman and Company, 1977). Ophuls proposes that our present civilization has outlived its usefulness and envisions a humane and moral alternative.

Lois Robbins, *Waking Up in the Age of Creativity* (Santa Fe: Bear & Co., 1985). An illumination of the vital relationship between creativity and spirituality. Robbins calls for the rediscovery of ourselves and the reunification of art, science, and religion, thus beginning the transformation of society.

Sidney B. Simon, *Vulture* (Niles, Ill.: Argus Communications, 1977). How to avoid putting down ourselves and others. Great for older children and young teens.

Brian Swimme, *The Universe Is a Green Dragon* (Santa Fe: Bear & Co., 1984). A presentation of contemporary physics that is both mystical and poetic. It shows that the dignity of the individual is affirmed as a significant part of the cosmos.

Listenings

The Christmas Revels, Revels, Inc., Box 502, Cambridge, MA 02139. The first of three joyous seasonal albums with traditional and ritual carols, dances, and processionals in celebration of the winter solstice.

Contacts

Amnesty International USA, 322 Eighth Ave., New York, NY 10001.

Fellowship of Reconciliation, Box 271, Nyack, NY 10960.

Food First, Institute for Food and Development Policy, 145 Ninth Street, San Francisco, CA 94103-3584.

Friends of Creation Spirituality, Inc., P.O. Box 19216, Oakland, CA 94619.

Global Education Associates, Suite 456, 475 Riverside Dr., New York, NY 10115.

Notes

Introduction

1. Peter Berger, *The Precarious Vision* (New York: Doubleday, 1961), p. 10.
2. Ibid., p. 11.

Chapter 1

1. Alvin Toffler, *Learning for Tomorrow* (New York: Vintage Books, 1974), p. 11.

Chapter 2

1. Michael Novak, *Choosing Our King* (New York: Macmillan, 1974), p. 118–122.
2. Newsletter, Clergy and Laity Concerned.
3. William Fulbright, *The Arrogance of Power* (New York: Random House, 1966), p. 245.
4. L. Harold DeWolf, *What Americans Should Do About Crime* (New York: Harper & Row, 1976), pp. 75–77.
5. W. L. Miller, *Of Thee, Nevertheless, I Sing* (New York: Harcourt, Brace, Jovanovich, 1975), p. 235.
6. James Sellers, *Warming Fires* (New York: Seabury, 1975), p. 94.
7. Ibid., p. 44.
8. Bruce Catton and William B. Catton, *The Bold and Magnificent Dream* (Garden City, N.Y.: Doubleday, 1978), p. 177.
9. Sellers, *Warming Fires,* p. 62.
10. Bruce Birch and Larry L. Rasmussen, *The Predicament of the Prosperous* (Philadelphia: Westminster Press, 1978), p. 49.
11. Ralph Barton Perry, *Puritanism and Democracy* (New York: Vanguard Press, 1944), p. 80.

Chapter 3

1. Erich Fromm, *To Have or to Be* (New York: Harper & Row, 1976), pp. 109–110.
2. Howard Thurman, *The Growing Edge* (New York: Harper & Row, 1956), p. 78.

Chapter 4

1. Gerald Mische and Patricia Mische, *Toward a Human World Order* (New York: Paulist Press, 1977), p. 23.
2. Alexis de Tocqueville, "The Tyranny of the Majority," in Richard L. Rapson, ed., *Individualism and Conformity in the American Character* (Lexington, Mass.: D.C. Heath, 1967), p. 4.
3. Harriet Martineau, "Conformity in the East and Individualism in the West," in Richard L. Rapson, ibid., p. 20.

Chapter 5

1. James H. Craig and Marge Craig, *Synergic Power* (Berkeley, Calif.: Proactive Press, 1974), p. 60.
2. Leonard Bickman, "Clothes Make the Person," *Psychology Today* (April 1974), pp. 49–51.
3. Erich Fromm, *To Have or to Be* (New York: Harper & Row, 1976), p. 27.
4. Daniel Yankelovich, *New Rules: Searching for Self-Fulfillment* (New York: Random House, 1981), p. 7.
5. Joanne McAllister, "The Dream of Good Work," *Creation,* vol. 2, no. 2 (May/June 1986), p. 33.
6. Dorothee Soelle, quoted in ibid.

Chapter 6

1. Matthew Fox, *Original Blessing* (Santa Fe: Bear & Co., 1983), p. 94.
2. Gabriele Uhlein, ed., *Meditations with Hildegard of Bingen* (Santa Fe: Bear & Co., 1983), p. 49.
3. Klaus Westermann, *Blessing* (Philadelphia: Fortress Press, 1978), p. 5.
4. Paul Tillich, *The Shaking of the Foundations* (New York: Charles Scribner's Sons, 1948), pp. 154–155.
5. Eloi Leclerc, quoted in Matthew Fox, *Original Blessing,* p. 120.
6. Matthew Fox, *A Spirituality Named Compassion* (Minneapolis: Winston Press, 1979), p. 89.
7. Gabriele Uhlein, ed., *Meditations with Hildegard of Bingen,* p. 50.
8. Fellowship of Reconciliation poster.

Chapter 7

1. Dietrich Bonhoeffer, *Ethics* (New York: Macmillan, 1975), pp. 248–254.

Chapter 8

1. James H. Craig and Marge Craig, *Synergic Power* (Berkeley, Calif.: Proactive Press, 1974), p. 62.
2. Paul Wiegand, "Escape from the Birdbath," in Philip N. Johnson and Ken Butigan, eds., *Cry of the Environment* (Santa Fe: Bear & Co., 1984), p. 153.
3. Ibid., p. 155.

4. Elizabeth Dodson Gray, *Green Paradise Lost* (Wellesley, Mass.: Roundtable Press, 1979), p. 140.

5. William Ophuls, *Ecology and the Politics of Scarcity* (San Francisco: W. H. Freeman, 1977), p. 242.

6. Eric Gill, quoted in Wendell Berry, *Home Economics* (San Francisco: North Point Press, 1987), p. 166.

7. Dorothy Soelle, quoted in Joanne McAllister, "The Dream of Good Work," *Creation,* vol. 2, no. 2 (May/June 1986), p. 33.

Chapter 9

1. William A. Williams, *America Confronts a Revolutionary World 1776–1976* (New York: William Morrow, 1976), p. 192.

2. Erich Fromm, *To Have or to Be* (New York: Harper & Row, 1976), p. 135.

3. H. Richard Niebuhr, *Radical Monotheism and Western Culture* (New York: Harper & Row, 1943), pp. 24–25.

4. Fustel de Coulanges, quoted in Will Herberg, "America's Civil Religion: What It Is and Whence It Came," in R. Richey and D. Jones, eds., *American Civil Religion* (New York: Harper & Row, 1974), p. 76.

5. Henri Frankfort, et al., *The Intellectual Adventure of Ancient Man* (Chicago: University of Chicago Press, 1946), p. 191.

6. Ibid., p. 186.

7. R. Lindner, "Civil Religion in Historical Perspective," in *The Journal of Church and State,* vol. 17, no. 3 (1975), p. 406.

8. Erich Fromm, *To Have or to Be,* p. 136.

Chapter 10

1. William Ophuls, *Ecology and the Politics of Scarcity* (San Francisco: W. H. Freeman, 1977), p. 159.

2. Alvin Toffler, *Future Shock* (New York: Bantam Books, 1970), p. 458.

3. Ibid., p. 452.

4. Quoted in William A. Williams, *America Confronts a Revolutionary World 1776–1976* (New York: William Morrow, 1976), p. 65.

5. Ivan Illich, in Joel Spring, *Education and the Rise of the Corporate State* (Boston: Beacon Press, 1972), p. x.

6. Dennis C. Pirages and Paul R. Ehrlich, *Ark II* (New York: Viking Press, 1974), p. 190.

7. Joel Spring, *Education and the Rise of the Corporate State,* p. 118.

8. Ibid., pp. 118–119.

9. Jules Henry, *Culture Against Man* (New York: Random House, 1965), p. 297.

10. C. Weinberg, *Education Is a Shuck* (New York: William Morrow, 1975), p. 29.

11. Ivan Illich, "Education: A Consumer Commodity and a Pseudo-Religion," *The Christian Century,* vol. 88, no. 50 (1971), p. 1465.

12. Jeffrey Shranck, *Snap, Crackle, and Popular Taste* (New York: Delta, 1978), pp. 20–21.

Chapter 11

1. Boyd C. Shafer, *Nationalism: Myth and Reality* (New York: Harcourt Brace Jovanovich, 1955), p. 149.
2. Robert Bellah, *The Broken Covenant* (New York: Seabury Press, 1975), chapter 2.
3. Quoted in William A. Williams, *America Confronts a Revolutionary World 1776–1976* (New York: William Morrow, 1976), p. 31.
4. Ibid., p. 35.
5. Ruth Miller Elson, *Guardians of Tradition* (Lincoln: University of Nebraska Press, 1974), p. 62.
6. Williams A. Williams, *America Confronts a Revolutionary World,* p. 35.

Chapter 12

1. William Fulbright, *The Arrogance of Power* (New York: Random House, 1966), p. 22.
2. Ibid., p. 21.

Chapter 13

1. Michael Shapiro, quoted in Anne Hayner, "A New Voice for an Old Vision: Toward an Alternative Language of Security," *Manchester College Bulletin of Peace Studies,* vol. 16, nos. 1 and 2 (1986), p. 11.
2. Anne Hayner, ibid., p. 16.

Also from Meyer • Stone Books...

NAMING THE IDOLS

Biblical Alternatives for U.S. Foreign Policy

Richard Shaull

Foreword by Richard Falk

"I would rather entrust the foreign policy of this country to Richard Shaull than to our present State Department, no matter which party is in the White House and regardless of who is selected to serve as Secretary of State.... Shaull offers us much wisdom with great clarity... a valuable and exhilarating book."

— Richard Falk, Center of International Studies,
Woodrow Wilson School for Public and International Affairs,
Princeton, New Jersey

"... a superb, even stunning job! Richard Shaull knows and understands the Bible, and brings it to bear with rare compassion and competence. I am a lifelong biblical scholar; but he leaves me in wonder at his gifts in opening my eyes to what I have failed to see, or failed to see clearly."

— B. Davie Napier, Professor of Bible,
Yale University, Emeritus

"Richard Shaull is ideally equipped to evaluate U.S. foreign policy in light of scriptural and especially prophetic teaching. He has worked for many years in Colombia, Brazil, and Central America. We have here the fire, the vision, and the wisdom of a true prophet."

— Gary MacEoin, author of *Sanctuary: A Resource Guide*

Richard Shaull is Henry Winter Luce Professor of Ecumenics, Emeritus, Princeton. For over forty-five years he has been involved in helping North Americans learn from and be changed by their encounter with Third World realities.

Social Concerns 160 pp.

Paperback: $9.95 (ISBN 0-940989-32-8)